THE
Mayo Clinic
Williams-Sonoma
COOKBOOK

THE
Mayo Clinic
Williams-Sonoma
COOKBOOK

SIMPLE SOLUTIONS FOR EATING WELL

recipe writer

John Phillip Carroll

photographer

Chris Shorten

TIME
LIFE
BOOKS

TIME-LIFE BOOKS

Time-Life Books is a division of Time Life Inc.

Time-Life is a trademark of Time Warner Inc. U.S.A.

TIME-LIFE CUSTOM PUBLISHING

Vice President and Publisher: Terry Newell

Managing Editor: Donia Ann Steele

Director of Acquisitions: Jennifer L. Pearce

Vice President of Sales and Marketing: Neil Levin

Director of Financial Operations: J. Brian Birky

MAYO CLINIC

Editor-in-Chief: Donald Hensrud, M.D., M.P.H.

Nutrition Editors: Nancy B. Kaufman, M.P.H., R.D., Jennifer Nelson, M.S., R.D.

Senior Editor for New Product Development: Nicole Spelhaug

Promotion Services Managers: Kristin Bjerke, Marne Gade

Corporate Communications: Suzanne Leaf-Brock

WILLIAMS-SONOMA

Founder and Vice Chairman: Chuck Williams

Book Buyer: Victoria Kalish

WELDON OWEN INC.

President: John Owen

Vice President and Publisher: Wendely Harvey

Chief Operating Officer: Larry Partington

Vice President International Sales: Stuart Laurence

Managing Editor: Jill Fox

Consulting Editor: Norman Kolpas

Editorial/Production Assistant: Cecily Upton

Recipe Consultant: Peggy Fallon

Copy Editor: Carolyn Miller

Production Director: Stephanie Sherman

Art Director: Diane Dempsey

Food and Prop Stylist: Heidi Gintner

Food Styling Assistant: Kim Konecny

Nutritional Analysis: Hill Nutrition Associates

Index: ALTA Indexing Service

Proofreaders: Kris Balloun, Linda Bouchard, Ken Dellapenta, Jennifer Zahgkuni

Illustrator: Nicole Kaufman

Props Courtesy: Sue Fisher King, Sandra Griswold, Williams-Sonoma

Conceived and produced by Weldon Owen Inc.
814 Montgomery Street, San Francisco, CA 94133

In collaboration with Williams-Sonoma
3250 Van Ness Avenue, San Francisco, CA 94109

Mayo Clinic, your source of reliable consumer health information.
Mayo Clinic Health Oasis
http://www.mayohealth.org
200 First Street SW, Rochester, MN 55905

Printed in China by Leefung-Asco Printers Ltd.

A Weldon Owen Production
Copyright ©1998 Weldon Owen Inc.
All rights reserved, including the right of reproduction in whole or in part in any form.
First printed in 1998
10 9 8 7 6 5 4 3 2 1
Library of Congress
Cataloging-in-Publication Data
Carroll, John Phillip.
The Mayo Clinic/Williams-Sonoma Cookbook:
Simple Solutions for Eating Well /
by John Phillip Carroll
     p. cm.
   Includes index.
   ISBN 0-7370-0008-2
   1. Cookery.   I. Mayo Clinic II. Title
TX714.C37317   1998
641.5—dc21   98-22188
                           CIP

A note on weights and measures
All recipes include customary U.S. and metric measurements. Metric conversions are based on a standard developed for this book and have been rounded off. Actual weights may vary.

A note on nutritional analysis
Each recipe is analyzed for significant nutrients per serving. Not included in the analysis are ingredients that are suggested as an alternative or substitution either in the recipe or in the recipe introduction or accompanying tip.

On the cover
For a stunning spring feast, pair entree Poached Salmon with Melon Salsa (recipe on page 215) and complement Potato Salad with Tarragon Vinaigrette (recipe on page 120). Finish with Multigrain Quick Bread (recipe on page 239).

our commitment

*t*his book is dedicated to the paramount belief that eating well is a pleasurable experience because good food tastes good and because it has important health benefits. Throughout these pages, Mayo Clinic, the world-renowned medical center, and Williams-Sonoma, the nation's leading cookware authority, join forces to offer you the ultimate guide for eating well: simple, healthful recipes to cook and enjoy.

Using common foods and simple cooking techniques, the recipes and their photographs on these pages provide bountiful evidence that nutrition is delicious. You will find foods brimming with bright colors and delightful textures. Once you try these Starters, Complements, Entrees, and Finishes recipes, you will soon discover another notable attribute: wonderful flavor. After reading the nutritional information in the Introduction to this book and preparing the food, you too will appreciate the health benefits and pleasures that come from eating well every day.

contents

*t*he decisions you make each day about selecting and preparing food affect how you feel today and how well you live in the years ahead. The information in this chapter is based on the contributions of an expert panel of Mayo Clinic physicians and registered dietitians in association with the food experts of Williams-Sonoma. Its practical, easy-to-use nutrition advice complies with current recommendations for Americans. The panel's goal was to help you answer the question: How do I eat well? The answer, presented here, is that eating well begins with enjoying a variety of foods that can help keep you healthy and prevent disease. Planning nutritionally balanced menus, shopping for the finest ingredients, and using healthful cooking techniques sum up the approach to eating well. The recipes that follow this introduction show you how easy and enjoyable eating well can be.

introduction

Finding pleasure in eating well

i f you figure eating well means counting calories or tallying fat grams, it's time to think about food in a new way. Eating well means enjoying great taste as well as great nutrition. Begin this new way of thinking by learning more about what food provides. Because your body is a complex machine, it needs a variety of foods to achieve a balanced mix of energy. That variety, emphasizing more whole grains, vegetables, and fruits and fewer animal foods, can lead to a diet that provides a rich supply of nutrients, fiber, and other substances associated with better health. In addition to these benefits, variety introduces you to myriad textures and flavors that boost your satisfaction and pleasure.

complement combination

Reach to an Asian influence for a spring meal made up of a variety of grain, vegetable, and fruit dishes. You can serve six people this three-course dinner after less than one hour in the kitchen. Begin with a simple salad, followed by a main course made up of two complement recipes using only grains and vegetables. You can stir-fry the vegetables while the rice steams. Finish this colorful meal with a stunning fruit parfait (above). For a complete recipe list and nutritional analysis of the Spring Menu, see page 19.

Eating Well Means Enjoying Variety

On the pages that follow is the latest information about how food can help keep you healthy. But the simple solution to eating well can be summarized in one word: variety. No one food provides all the nutrients your body needs. A variety of foods helps ensure the right mix of nutrients for health.

Choose a variety of foods. For better health and enjoyable meals, choose from a variety of grains, vegetables, legumes, fruits, dairy products, poultry, seafood, and lean meats. Each of these food groups provides unique combinations of nutrients. Variety also allows you to balance a few higher fat, higher calorie foods with lower fat, lower calorie ones.

Plan meals around small portions of a variety of foods. Within each food group there is an array of foods, offering a variety of nutrients, colors, textures, and flavors. Following recommended serving sizes makes it easy to enjoy variety while maintaining a healthy weight.

Shop for a variety of fresh foods at peak quality. Look for fresh foods in season for maximum flavor at minimum cost. Make planning, shopping for, and cooking healthful meals a family activity. Youngsters, for example, might enjoy researching ingredients on food labels, joining you on trips to the farmers' market, or helping you prepare new recipes from this book.

Cook foods using a variety of healthful techniques. You don't have to learn intricate procedures or buy any special pieces of equipment to cook well. Healthful cooking techniques are simply standard cooking methods designed to enhance foods' natural qualities without adding unnecessary calories, fat, or sodium.

using this book

The recipes in this book were designed using a wide variety of foods. Equal importance was given to the nutrients food should provide a healthy body and the pleasure good-tasting food should bring.

All of the recipes were also designed with an eye toward ease, starting with the use of only commonly available ingredients. You should be able to find all the ingredients for every recipe in this book in any well-stocked supermarket. Ingredients are listed in order of use in the step-by-step method. The recipe introduction gives seasonal substitutions and serving suggestions. The majority of the recipes serve six people. Check each for its specific yield. Preparation and cooking times are provided as a guide for today's busy cooks.

The photographs that accompany the recipes show you the food cooked exactly as the recipe is written. When a single serving is presented, it is exactly the amount of food designed to serve one person, as recorded in the nutritional analysis.

An important feature of each recipe appears at its conclusion: a per-serving analysis of calories, protein, carbohydrates, total fat, saturated fat, cholesterol, sodium, and dietary fiber.

The Nutrition Notes, paired with many recipes, contain useful information from Mayo Clinic about a recipe's impact on your health. Other recipes feature Cooking Clinics from the experts at Williams-Sonoma: quick discussions of easy techniques for choosing, storing, or preparing specific foods.

The index, which begins on page 270, is your guide to main ingredients, nutritional terms, and features. The chapters are organized to make it easy to plan menus for eating well.

introduction

This opening chapter outlines what you need to know to eat well. It provides simple information about the important role food plays in general health and in preventing disease. Then, it describes how to get the most out of your food, in learning how to plan meals, choose ingredients, and easily prepare all of the wondrous recipes that follow.

starters

The first recipe chapter features appetizers, soups, and salads. Use these in their traditional way, to begin a meal, or make up an entire meal by serving two or three of these dishes together.

complements

The next chapter includes many recipes for what might ordinarily be termed side dishes: vegetable, grain, potato, and pasta dishes that can complement a main-course recipe. You can also eat these recipes alone as a light meal, use them as a single course within a larger meal, or combine several for a meal full of delightful tastes, textures, shapes, and colors.

entrees

These dishes fulfill the more familiar main-course role, but there is a difference here as well: Grains, vegetables, and fruits take on leading roles, while meat, poultry, and seafood play supporting roles.

finishes

Finally comes an interesting selection of beautiful, flavorful drinks, breads, and desserts to round out a meal. Enjoy the drinks with food or between meals. Many of the baked goods also make outstanding breakfast pastries. Again, grains and fruits dominate the recipes.

Meeting daily food goals

Over the years, nutrition guidelines have evolved to keep pace with advances in nutrition knowledge. During the last fifty years, nutrition experts have developed a better understanding of how diet influences general health as well as its role in preventing chronic diseases. Research suggests that regularly eating a variety of foods is your best bet for maintaining health and reducing your risk of disease. The recommendations presented here are for healthy people two years and older. If the food goals seem to be a lot to eat every day, notice the serving sizes on the opposite page. Each group offers an assortment of foods with rather modest portions.

refreshing repast

Enjoy the fresh favorites of summer, including nutrient-rich tomatoes, zucchini, and straw-berries, in this delightfully quick meal, designed to keep you out of the kitchen as much as possible. You can make everything ahead for this dinner for eight, and serve it warm or cold. This complete menu, including the cool dessert above, is just 611 calories (2,558 kilojoules). For a complete recipe list and nutritional analysis of the Summer Menu, see page 19.

Grains: 6 to 11 servings
All grains—cereals, breads, rice, and pasta—are rich in complex carbohydrates and provide a variety of nutrients. Despite a common misconception that breads and pasta are fattening, these foods are low in fat and calories. Along with vegetables and fruits, grains should form the foundation of your diet every day. Choose whole grains frequently because they contain more fiber than refined grains.

Vegetables: At least 3 servings
Vegetables are low in calories and virtually fat-free, while providing a variety of vitamins, minerals, and in most cases, fiber. In addition, vegetables contain phytochemicals, substances that can reduce your risk of cardiovascular disease and some cancers.

Fruits: At least 2 servings
All fruit in any form—fresh, dried, frozen, and canned—plays an important role in eating well. Along with the benefits of few calories, little or no fat, vitamins, minerals, phytochemicals, and dietary fiber, fruits serve as natural sweeteners to other foods.

Legumes: Frequently as alternatives to animal foods
Low in fat and with no cholesterol, legumes—beans, dried peas, and lentils—are your best source of plant protein. They also provide nutrients, phytochemicals, and dietary fiber.

Dairy Products: 2 to 3 servings
Milk, yogurt, and cheese are outstanding sources of calcium and vitamin D, which helps your body absorb calcium. They also provide protein. However, dairy products can be high in fat and cholesterol, so lowfat or nonfat products are your best choices.

Poultry, Seafood, and Meat: No more than 3 servings
Poultry, seafood, and meat are rich sources of protein, with B vitamins, iron, and zinc. However, because even lean varieties contain fat and cholesterol, limit all animal foods.

Eggs: No more than 4 eggs a week
While eggs provide protein and iron, each yolk contains about 200 milligrams of cholesterol, or two thirds of the daily recommended limit for healthy adults. When counting eggs, include those used in baking. Cholesterol-free egg products and egg whites can replace whole eggs in most recipes (see page 231).

Fats, Sweets, and Alcohol: Sparingly
The fats and sugars that occur naturally in certain foods provide calories with no nutrients. To eat well, cook foods with little or no oil or other fats and limit sweets such as candy, sugar-sweetened soft drinks, and many desserts. If you choose to drink alcohol, limit yourself to 1 drink a day if you're a nonpregnant woman and two drinks a day if you're a man.

determining a serving

grains

1/2 cup (3 oz/90 g) cooked cereal, rice, or pasta

1/2 cup (1 oz/30 g) ready-to-eat cereal

1 4-inch (10-cm) pancake

1 slice whole wheat (wholemeal) sandwich bread

1/2 bagel or English muffin

2 cups air-popped popcorn

vegetables and fruits

1 cup (2 oz/60 g) raw leafy green vegetables

1/2 cup (3 oz/90 g) cooked vegetables

1 medium potato

1/2 cup (3 oz/90 g) applesauce

1/4 cup (1 1/2 oz/45 g) raisins

3/4 cup (6 fl oz/180 ml) 100% fruit juice

1 medium apple or banana

12 grapes

dairy products

1 cup (8 fl oz/250 ml) lowfat or nonfat milk or yogurt

1 1/2 oz (45 g) reduced-fat or nonfat cheese

2 cups (16 oz/500 g) lowfat or nonfat cottage cheese

poultry, seafood, meat

2–3 oz (60–90 g) cooked skinless poultry, seafood, or lean meat

meat alternatives

Each of these counts as 1 ounce (30 g) of meat:

1/2 cup (3 1/2 oz/105 g) cooked legumes

1 egg

2 tablespoons peanut butter

1/4 cup (1 oz/30 g) seeds

1/3 cup (1 oz/30 g) nuts

1/2 cup (4 oz/125 g) tofu

Understanding nutritional goals

b y learning more about how your body uses the nutrients different foods provide, you'll better understand how eating well affects your health. Every recipe in this book is accompanied by a nutritional analysis calculated by a registered dietitian. The recipes are analyzed according to eight markers: calories, protein, carbohydrates, total fat, saturated fat, cholesterol, sodium, and dietary fiber. A daily nutritional goal for each of these markers is provided below. Too much or too little of these substances has a great impact on your health. Use these recommendations as a guide when planning your daily meals and snacks.

Calories: 1,600 to 2,800 a day

The calorie is a measurement of the amount of energy provided by a food or recipe. Kilojoules is an alternative term used in some countries, with 1 calorie equal to 4.2 kilojoules.

The average calories required by an adult is 2,000 (8,400 kilojoules) per day. However, most women and some older adults need just 1,600 (6,700 kilojoules); most men, active women, teenage girls, and children should have about 2,200 (9,240 kilojoules); and active men and teenage boys about 2,800 (11,760 kilojoules). For general health and better weight control, try to distribute calories evenly throughout the day.

Protein: About 12 percent of calories

Your body uses protein to make and maintain tissues such as muscles and organs. However, most Americans typically eat far more protein than they need. A high-protein diet is typically high in fat and cholesterol.

You can get protein from a variety of sources. Legumes, poultry, seafood, meat, dairy products, nuts, and seeds are your richest sources of protein. Grains and vegetables supply small amounts. In a 2,000-calorie diet, 12 percent of calories from protein is 60 grams. Even if you don't eat any animal protein, you can easily get enough protein as long as you eat a variety of foods that provide enough calories to maintain your healthy weight.

Carbohydrates: 55 to 65 percent of calories

Foods high in carbohydrates are used mostly for energy. Complex carbohydrates are the starches and fibers in grains, vegetables, and legumes. Simple carbohydrates are the sugars in sweets, fruits, and milk. Try to eat most of your carbohydrates as complex carbohydrates. Your body absorbs complex carbohydrates more slowly than simple sugars for a more continuous energy supply. Complex carbohydrates also provide more nutrients and fiber than do sweets.

Fat: 20 to 30 percent of calories

Fat is your most concentrated energy source. The kinds of fat in foods include saturated, polyunsaturated, trans fatty acids (trans fats), and monounsaturated.

Major sources of saturated fat are butter, cheese, whole milk and cream, meat, poultry, chocolate, coconut, palm oil, lard, and solid shortenings. Most vegetable oils contain polyunsaturated fat. When vegetable oil is hydrogenated to form margarine or shortening, trans fats are formed. Olive and canola oils and nuts contain mainly monounsaturated fat.

Saturated and trans fats increase the risk of coronary artery disease by raising blood cholesterol levels. High blood levels of cholesterol can lead to narrowing of your arteries and an increased risk of heart attack and stroke. Polyunsaturated fats lower blood cholesterol, but also seem to be susceptible to oxidation. Oxidation is a process that enables cells in your arteries to absorb fats and cholesterol. Over time, oxidation speeds the buildup of plaque that narrows arteries. Monounsaturated fats may help lower blood cholesterol and are resistant to oxidation. Control calories from all fats. Based on a 2,000-calorie diet, limit fat to a maximum of 65 grams. When you do use fat, try to choose monounsaturated sources such as olive oil. Using oils in place of margarine also minimizes trans fats.

Saturated Fat: No more than 10 percent of total calories
Although both trans and saturated fats raise blood cholesterol levels, foods containing saturated fats are more prevalent in typical diets. As you limit fat, minimize the portion that is saturated.

Cholesterol: No more than 300 milligrams a day
All foods made from animals contain cholesterol. Concentrated sources include organ meats, egg yolks, and whole milk products.

The primary dietary determinant of high blood cholesterol is saturated fat. For some people however, dietary cholesterol can raise the level of blood cholesterol higher.

Sodium: No more than 2,400 milligrams a day
Sodium occurs naturally in foods. It also makes up 40 percent of table salt (sodium chloride). You need only a small amount of sodium—less than one-quarter teaspoon of salt—to help regulate fluid balance. Too much sodium may contribute to a rise in blood pressure, putting you at risk for heart attack and stroke.

Control sodium by limiting processed foods. Also, cut back on the salt you add to food in cooking and at the table. At first, lessening salt may cause your food to taste bland. That is because your taste buds have become accustomed to it. As you use less salt, your preference for salt will lessen, allowing you to enjoy the taste of the food itself.

Dietary Fiber: 20 to 35 grams a day
Dietary fiber is largely plant cell material that resists digestion. Insoluble fiber moves through your digestive system quickly, helping prevent constipation and reducing your risk of colon cancer. It's found mainly in vegetables, wheat bran, and whole grains. Soluble fiber may help improve blood cholesterol levels and blood sugar control. Generous amounts are found in oats, legumes, and fruits.

The best way to boost fiber is to eat a variety of whole grains, vegetables, legumes, and fruits. When buying breads or grains, look for the word "whole" on the label.

reading a nutritional analysis

Every recipe in this book is accompanied by an analysis performed by a registered dietitian.

Every ingredient listed for use in the recipe is included in the analysis. Subrecipes are analyzed both as they are served in the main recipe and on their own in the portion indicated. For example, the baked goods are analyzed by item and sauces by tablespoon.

The measurements are rounded for easier reading. Amounts between 0 and 1 are listed as <1 (less than one). Alternative ingredients, suggestions in the recipe introductions, and accompaniments in the photographs are not included. Remember, a serving for the recipe and analysis is not necessarily a serving as defined by your daily food goals.

Reducing your risk of disease

*Y*ou can't overcome the impact your age or family history has on your health. But information continues to point out how a healthy lifestyle can improve and, in some cases, eliminate significant risk factors for several chronic conditions. Eating well, not smoking, exercising regularly, and maintaining a healthy weight are sound strategies you can adopt now to reduce your risk of chronic disease and improve the quality of your life. A varied diet based on grains, vegetables, legumes, and fruits is low in fat and high in fiber. In addition, plant foods contain a variety of substances that may help prevent the chronic conditions listed below as well as obesity, kidney stones, and gallstones.

Combat Coronary Artery Disease

Limiting saturated fat to no more than 10 percent of total calories, total fat to 20 to 30 percent of daily calories, and dietary cholesterol to 300 milligrams daily, along with exercise, can control your blood cholesterol level. Of these, limiting saturated fat is the most important step to reducing your blood cholesterol level and risk of coronary artery disease.

Eating fish may protect against coronary artery disease because it contains omega-3 fatty acids. These fats may help lower your triglyceride level (another type of blood fat). They also may help lower blood pressure slightly and help thin your blood to reduce your risk of clots. Blood clots that form in narrowed arteries increase your risk of heart attack or stroke.

Eating more foods with soluble fiber, such as oats and legumes, also may lead to small decreases in your blood cholesterol level.

Antioxidants that occur in your body and some foods may block some of the damage caused by oxidation. This damage may contribute to narrowing of your arteries.

Although fortifying foods with folic acid (folate) is primarily designed to prevent spinal cord birth defects, adequate folic acid may reduce the amount of homocysteine (an amino acid that builds and maintains tissues) in your blood. Too much homocysteine can increase your risk of heart attack, stroke, or peripheral vascular disease (loss of circulation in hands and feet).

Help Prevent Cancer

Eating more fruits and vegetables is one of the most important things you can do to protect against cancer.

Fiber may help reduce your risk of colon cancer. Green and dark-yellow vegetables, beans, soybean products, and cruciferous vegetables (broccoli, cauliflower, cabbage) may reduce your risk of colon and stomach cancer.

Eating more plant foods can leave less room for the kinds of foods, such as fatty meats, that may increase your risk of cancer. Eating too much saturated fat, in particular, is likely linked to a higher risk of colon cancer and probably prostate cancer. Fat's relationship to breast cancer is inconsistent. Also, excess calories from fat can lead to obesity, a risk factor for several cancers.

Avoiding alcohol may reduce your risk of cancers of the mouth, esophagus, larynx, and probably breast.

Lower Blood Pressure

High blood pressure is one of the leading causes of stroke, heart attack, congestive heart failure, kidney failure, and premature death. Exercising regularly, eating plenty of fruits and vegetables, limiting sodium and alcohol, and maintaining a healthy weight can help reduce or prevent high blood pressure.

Control Diabetes

Among adults with diabetes, more than 90 percent have type 2 diabetes. The greatest risk factor for type 2 diabetes is obesity.

The keys to a healthy weight are eating well and exercising regularly. Eating plenty of whole grains, legumes, vegetables, and fruits can make it easier to limit calories. The fiber in these foods may also help control blood sugar. Having diabetes increases your risk of cardiovascular disease, making control of calories from fat and cholesterol even more important.

finding disease protection in food

Most of the nutrients and other substances associated with better health are found in plentiful amounts in grains, vegetables, legumes, and fruits.

antioxidants

Antioxidant vitamins may help block cell damage caused by toxic molecules called free radicals. Damage from free radicals may contribute to diseases including cardiovascular disease and cancer. Look for antioxidants mainly in vegetables and fruits. Important antioxidants are vitamins C and E and carotenoids.

Vitamin C acts as an antioxidant to reduce the risk of cardiovascular disease, cataracts, and some cancers. Vitamin C abounds in green and red bell peppers (capsicums), collard greens, broccoli, spinach, tomatoes, potatoes, strawberries, oranges, and other citrus fruits.

Of all the antioxidants, vitamin E shows the most promise for protecting against cardiovascular disease. Rich sources include vegetable oils (such as soybean, corn, cottonseed, and safflower) and the products made from them. Wheat germ and nuts also contain relatively high amounts.

You may have heard of beta-carotene, perhaps the most commonly known of the carotenoids. However, beta-carotene represents less than 30 percent of all of the carotenoids in your blood. Population studies suggest that diets rich in several carotenoids supplied by a variety of fruits and vegetables may protect against cardiovascular disease, cataracts, and some cancers. Find carotenoids in deep-yellow, dark-green, and red vegetables and fruits including carrots, winter squash, sweet potatoes, spinach, broccoli, bell peppers (capsicums), tomatoes, papayas, cantaloupe, mangoes, apricots, and watermelon.

calcium

Calcium builds bones and teeth. In adults, eating too little calcium is linked with osteoporosis, a condition characterized by weak and brittle bones. Dairy products are your richest sources of calcium. If you don't or can't drink milk, legumes, some leafy green vegetables (including collard and turnip greens and broccoli) and calcium-fortified products are other ways to boost calcium.

folic acid

Folic acid (folate) may help during pregnancy to prevent spinal cord birth defects. Folic acid is also linked to possible cardiovascular benefits and cancer protection. You'll find folic acid in fortified cereals, beans and lentils, dark-green leafy vegetables, and citrus fruits.

omega-3 fatty acids

This type of polyunsaturated fat seems to positively influence a number of factors related to protection from cardiovascular disease. You'll find omega-3's mainly in fish, particularly in fatty, cold-water types such as salmon, mackerel, and herring. Lesser amounts are contained in soybeans, nuts, and flax seed.

phytochemicals

Experts believe hundreds of chemicals occur naturally in plants. Foods being studied for their possible health benefits include: garlic and onions (allium compounds); soybeans (phytoestrogens); grapes and peanuts (resveratrol and phenols); citrus fruits (limonene); cruciferous vegetables (sulforaphane and isothiocyanates); chile peppers (capsaisin); and green tea (polyphenols and catechins).

dietary fiber

In addition to the protection fiber may offer against cardiovascular disease and colon cancer, fiber helps prevent constipation. Foods contain two types of fiber: insoluble and soluble fibers. Insoluble fiber is mainly in whole grains. Soluble fiber is contained in oats, dried beans, and some fruits.

antioxidants

The vegetable and juice in Broccoli in Spicy Orange Sauce provide vitamin C and beta carotene.

RECIPE ON PAGE 96

folic acid

Salads of leafy greens and citrus, such as Minted Mediterranean Fruit Mix, supply this B vitamin.

RECIPE ON PAGE 51

omega-3 fatty acids

The fish in Poached Salmon with Melon Salsa is one of the best sources of omega-3's.

RECIPE ON PAGE 215

dietary fiber

This serving of legumes in Quick Baked Beans with Carrot Relish provides 9 grams of fiber.

RECIPE ON PAGE 159

Planning meals for eating well

*n*o single recipe or individual meal can provide all the nutrients you need. As the information on the preceding pages illustrates, the best way to promote health and protect yourself from disease is by eating a variety of different foods regularly. You also need to consider who you are cooking for and the time you have to cook. Every meal brings you the opportunity to plan menus featuring a variety of seasonal vegetables and fruits, legumes, and whole grains. One of the easiest ways to ensure variety is to plan meals around a range of food colors and textures. If you use the basic principle of variety as your guide, you can't help but enjoy the benefits of eating well.

Useful Tools for Meal Planning

As you try to meet the daily food and nutritional goals outlined on the previous pages, remember these points for planning healthful meals:

Enjoy variety, balance, and moderation. Variety means eating from several different food groups. It also means choosing a variety of foods from within each group. As you try new foods, remember every food you eat does not need to be an excellent source of nutrients and fiber. Nor is it out of the question to eat high-fat or high-calorie foods occasionally. Simply put, balance means choosing foods that promote your health more often than those that don't. Moderation means not eating too much or too little of any one food. It also means eating the right amount of calories to achieve or maintain your healthy weight.

Consider your diners' needs. Always keep in mind the people who will be eating the meal. Children and older adults have typically smaller appetites than the average adult, for example. When planning a menu for people outside your immediate family, verify any special health needs including pregnancy, food allergies, and chronic diseases such as diabetes.

Lifestyle choices, cultural preferences, and individual likes and dislikes have a huge impact on everyone's enjoyment of a meal. Athletes tend to need more calories than sedentary folks, and vegetarians will appreciate your planning a meatless meal. For religious reasons, some people prefer not to eat certain foods. And some people are simply wary of different foods. If you are introducing new ingredients and cooking techniques, begin by pairing new foods with familiar favorites. This will make it easier for some people to adjust to the changes eating well may create.

Pay attention to the season. The time of year will tell you what fresh produce is best in the markets, such as asparagus in spring, tomatoes in summer, hard-shelled squashes in autumn, or oranges in winter. Not only will you be buying the best fruits and vegetables available, in many cases you'll save money by purchasing locally grown fresh produce.

Of course, the seasons bring special holidays that call for their own traditional ingredients. This is also a good opportunity to serve a traditional food prepared in a new way or to introduce a new, more healthful recipe into a traditional meal.

Know your time limits. Your time to prepare a meal is paramount to its success. Ultimately, you need to find as much satisfaction in a meal's preparation as in its consumption. The recipes in this book include preparation and cooking times that will help you in this organizing process.

Make a pretty plate. When you plan any menu, choose recipes that offer a complementary array of colors, shapes, textures, and aromas. Such a varied selection of foods on your plate is sure to delight the senses. It is also a simple process for menu planning as a colorful variety provides a greater selection of nutrients. The four menu styles presented at right are some ideas of how a menu varies depending on how your meal will be served.

Simplify your goals. Refer to pages 12 and 13 to plan menus based on recommended daily amounts of food and pages 14 and 15 to help you reach your nutritional goals. However, don't let eating well become a number-crunching chore. Simply eat more grains, vegetables, legumes, and fruits, and fewer animal foods, fats, and sweets. Over time, this approach will help ensure eating well for you and your family.

putting together menus

Spring

complement combination

Spicy Spring Greens Salad

Sesame Asparagus-
and-Carrot Stir-fry

Saffron Rice
and Golden Raisin Pilaf

Fancy Fruit Parfaits

SERVES: 6 | PER SERVING

Calories....................................730
Kilojoules 3,054
Protein ....22 g
Carbohydrates ....129 g
Total Fat ....17 g
Saturated Fat ....2 g
Cholesterol ....3 mg
Sodium ....719 mg
Dietary Fiber...........................10 g
Calories from Fat 21%

PHOTO ON PAGE 10

RECIPES ON PAGES 43, 68, 111, 248

Summer

refreshing repast

Tomato and Walnut
Flat Bread

Spinach Salad
with Raspberry Vinaigrette

Zucchini Soup

Strawberry Shiver
and Kiwi Topping

SERVES: 8 | PER SERVING

Calories....................................611
Kilojoules 2,558
Protein ....18 g
Carbohydrates ....114 g
Total Fat ....10 g
Saturated Fat ....1 g
Cholesterol............................30 mg
Sodium ....550 mg
Dietary Fiber...........................14 g
Calories from Fat 15%

PHOTO ON PAGE 12

RECIPES ON PAGES 231, 47, 60, 256

Autumn

one-dish meal

Steamed Vegetables
with Roasted Pepper Sauce

Black Bean Chili
over Soft Polenta

Roasted Pineapple
with Raspberry Sauce

SERVES: 6 | PER SERVING

Calories....................................660
Kilojoules 2,761
Protein ....30 g
Carbohydrates ....129 g
Total Fat ....8 g
Saturated Fat ....<1 g
Cholesterol............................<1 mg
Sodium ....182 mg
Dietary Fiber...........................19 g
Calories from Fat 10%

PHOTO ON PAGE 20

RECIPES ON PAGES 39, 168, 267

Winter

traditional pairings

Gingered Carrot Soup

Lemon Zest Spinach

Rosemary Lamb
and
White Beans

Tropical-Fruit Crisps

SERVES: 6 | PER SERVING

Calories....................................840
Kilojoules 3,516
Protein ....43 g
Carbohydrates ....130 g
Total Fat ....20 g
Saturated Fat ....6 g
Cholesterol............................62 mg
Sodium ....684 mg
Dietary Fiber...........................18 g
Calories from Fat 21%

PHOTO ON PAGE 26

RECIPES ON PAGES 63, 88, 216, 260

Taking a fresh approach to shopping

*b*ecause eating well doesn't mean that you have to rely on hard-to-find or unusual foods, you do not have to drastically change the way you shop to find all the ingredients you need to cook the recipes in this book. Everything you need should be available in the average well-stocked supermarket. Of course, you may wish to expand your shopping options to give yourself an even greater variety of high-quality food. Where ever you shop, planning your meals and snacks first will make your trip faster and easier. At the store, understanding the current terminology and carefully reading the labels will help you make better decisions about packaged foods.

one-dish meal

This easy-to-make autumn dinner is perfect for busy weeknights. When shopping for polenta, look for packages labeled "polenta," the Italian term, and also those marked "cornmeal," as they are the same product. High in fiber, this hearty vegetarian meal for six has very little fat: including the fruit dessert (above), the menu comes in with only 8 grams. For a complete recipe list and nutritional analysis of the Autumn Menu, see page 19.

Savvy Shopping Strategies

These simple strategies can help you shop wisely:

Plan ahead. Before you go shopping, decide how many major meals you are going to buy for in this shopping trip. Then, think through the number of other food items you will need for breakfasts, lunches, and snacks in that time period. Take an inventory of your staples.

Make a shopping list. A list will make your shopping trip more efficient and help you avoid impulse purchases. If you generally shop in the same store, write a master list, with items you normally buy in the order that you travel through the store. Make copies to use during each shopping adventure, just adding items specifically for the recipes you plan to make.

Add to the list an indulgence—perhaps one favorite dessert, a food with a short season, or a new convenience item. Don't let a list prevent you from looking for and trying new foods.

Don't shop when you are hungry. It is harder to resist quick snacks when you need something to eat. These packaged foods are often high in calories, fat, and sodium. If you do find yourself shopping on an empty stomach, drink some water or buy a piece of fruit to munch on while you shop.

Broaden your sources. While you can find good food at markets you've always used, consider shopping at farmers' markets and specialty-food stores or by catalog as a way of bringing greater variety to your table.

Don't make shopping difficult. From time to time, personal convenience is a more important consideration than pristine quality. You can use frozen and canned produce in place of fresh for cooked recipes. Although the taste may not compare to fresh, there is little difference in most of the nutrients they offer. The same is true of some prepared items called for in several recipes in this book, including applesauce, prune purée, tomato purée, and sandwich bread. You can make them yourself, but a prepared version will in no way diminish the quality of the dishes.

Be an informed shopper. Talk to store personnel for advice on the best quality available. For packaged goods, learn the packaging terminology and read the food labels. If you don't always have time, choose one item at each shopping trip. For example, read the labels of ready-to-eat cereals, looking for whole grains in the ingredient lists and comparing fiber amounts among brands. Soon, you'll know the foods to buy without spending time reading all the labels all the time.

reading food labels

Most packaged foods carry label terms, which are also used in advertising, the ingredient list, and the nutrition facts.

label terms

Here is a sampling of common terms used on packaged foods.

Cholesterol-Free: To be listed as cholesterol-free, a product must have less than 2 milligrams of cholesterol and 2 grams (or less) of saturated fat per serving.

Fat-Free: Less than 0.5 grams of fat per serving.

Low-Calorie: Must contain 40 calories or less per serving.

Lowfat: The product contains 3 grams of fat or less per serving.

Lean: Packaged seafood, game meat, or cooked meat or poultry with less than 10 grams of fat, 4.5 grams or less of saturated fat, and no more than 95 milligrams of cholesterol per serving.

Light or Lite: The product contains one-third fewer calories than the original version; or no more than half the fat of the original; or no more than half the sodium of the original.

Reduced-Calorie: At least 25 percent fewer calories per serving than a similar food.

ingredient list

Food manufacturers are required to list all of the ingredients used in the product by weight from the most to the least.

nutrition facts

Since May 1994, packaged food sold in the United States has listed Nutrition Facts. Presented in a standard format on most labels, the Nutrition Facts are an at-a-glance method for verifying how a food fits into your plan of eating well.

Daily Food Values: These values represent the maximum amounts of nutrients and fiber desirable for 2,000-calorie (8,400-kilo-joule) and 2,500-calorie (10,500-kilojoule) diets.

Serving Sizes: If you eat more or less than the listed serving, be sure to adjust the nutrition information accordingly.

Nutrients: For the most part, the nutrients listed on food labels are the same as those shown in the nutritional analysis in this book (see page 15). In addition, food companies must list sugars, vitamins A and C, calcium, and iron. More nutrients may be listed on some labels.

Calories from Fat: Eating well means limiting fat to no more than 30 percent of calories. Remember, however, it's the total amount of fat you eat over time, and not the amount in one food or meal, that's important.

Using vegetables and fruits

*W*hether you enjoy them raw or cooked, on their own, or as embellishments for other dishes, vegetables and fruits offer a wide spectrum of pleasure. Of course, they provide nutrients, fiber, and other substances with few calories to promote your health. But in terms of eating well, don't forget their huge contribution in adding flavors, textures, and colors to your meals. Both vegetables and fruits can take the lead in soups, salads, and appetizers, as well as being used in breads, complements, and even entree dishes. Many robust vegetables have the potential to take a starring role in main dishes, and fruits can end a meal in stellar fashion.

Vegetables

Enjoy vegetables throughout the day. Fresh vegetables are best, but packaged versions can have comparable nutritional benefits.

Choose in-season vegetables. The closer you are to the growing source, the fresher your produce will be. Look for brightly colored vegetables. Your best items have blemish-free surfaces and regular, characteristic shapes and sizes. Leaves or greens should be crisp and free of wilting. Buy only the fresh vegetables you plan to eat within a few days. Long storage time diminishes nutrient levels and taste. Sort through and discard any damaged items. Bruises and nicks can attract molds, which can lead to spoilage of an entire bag of vegetables.

Store vegetables properly. Do not wash vegetables before storing. Place root vegetables in a cool, dark place. Store other vegetables in the refrigerator. Make sure all produce is dry before storing. Before cooking, wash vegetables well to remove dirt and pesticide residue. Wipe mushrooms clean with a damp cloth. Whenever possible, leave edible peels on vegetables. The peels of many vegetables—especially potatoes—contain considerable nutrients and dietary fiber.

ENHANCING foods with spices and herbs adds flavor without fat to many dishes. To store fresh herbs, trim the stems and place them in a glass of water like a bouquet of fresh flowers. Store dried herbs in tightly covered jars, away from light, at a cool room temperature. Use a mortar and pestle to grind spices just before adding to recipes.

BRAISING, also called simmering, cooks foods in a liquid medium in a nonstick frying pan on top of the stove. Sometimes the liquid comes from the ingredients themselves, such as the juices that ooze from the fruit during cooking in this recipe for Fragrant Fennel in Fresh Fig Sauce (recipe on page 95).

Enjoy packaged vegetables when out of season. Excellent examples of frozen produce are artichoke hearts, corn, peas, and lima beans. Some frozen vegetables, processed quickly after picking, offer more nutrients than less-than-peak-condition fresh vegetables. Look for canned vegetables without added salt.

Cook vegetables as quickly as possible. Long exposure to higher temperatures leads to loss of some nutrients. Consider reserving the cooking water, which can contain some nutrients, for adding to soups, stews, or sauces.

Fruits

Fresh fruit is always best, but dried, frozen, and fruits canned in their own juice or water are good alternatives.

Choose in-season fruits. Select fruits that feel heavy for their size. Heaviness is a good sign of juiciness. Smell fruits for characteristic aromas. Remember, if it smells peachy, it is peachy.

Use dried fruits sparingly. Buy dried fruits processed without added sugar. Dried fruits are a concentrated source of dietary fiber, but are also higher in calories than fresh fruit. Even dried fruits should be moist. Select dried fruits that are plump and avoid items that appear hard or smell of mold.

Read labels on packaged fruits. Many frozen fruits come in several varieties, processed with syrup, juice, or nothing at all. Look for frozen fruits processed plain without added sugar. Choose commercial canned fruit processed in water or fruit juice. Avoid fruits canned in sugar-sweetened syrup, which is a source of calories without nutrients.

Freeze seasonal fruits. You can freeze many fruits yourself, especially berries (see page 256).

Prepare fresh fruit close to serving time. To maximize flavor, texture, and nutrients, prepare fruit within about 1 hour of serving. Some salads benefit from a little chilling time for the various flavors to marry. Before cutting or eating whole, wash all fruits thoroughly under cold running water, including those with hard shells or skins such as melons. Wash your hands before and after handling fresh fruits.

Leave on edible peels. The peels of apples, pears, and most stone fruits are perfectly edible. They'll add interesting texture to recipes and contain extra nutrients and fiber.

Zest citrus peels. Before discarding citrus peels, remove their zest, the thin, brightly colored outermost layer. Grated or shredded, it adds a bright spark of flavor and color enhancement to both sweet and savory dishes.

enjoying more vegetables and fruits

Beyond the obvious ways you can enjoy vegetables and fruits, try these ideas for making it easier to reach your goals of eating at least three vegetables and two fruits every day:

- Add fresh or dried fruit to breakfast cereals.
- Include grated raw vegetables or dried fruit to batters and doughs for quick breads, muffins, and cookies.
- Replace the oil in baked goods with thick fruit purées such as applesauce (recipe on page 232) or prunes (recipe on page 236).
- Choose a wide variety of salad greens, including arugula, chicory, collards, dandelion greens, kale, mustard greens, spinach, and watercress.
- Look for pasta made with vegetables such as spinach or beets.
- Stir-fry vegetables with tofu or just a small portion of poultry, seafood, or meat.
- Use vegetables as a base for, or as added ingredients, in soups.
- Replace oil for sautéing with juice.
- Enrich and thicken soups and sauces with cooked and puréed vegetables in place of cream or whole milk.
- Add grated raw carrot or apple to lean ground beef or turkey when making meat loaf or meatballs.
- Make fruit sauces and toppings for desserts or pancakes.
- Drink 100% fruit juice mixed with sparkling water instead of soda.
- Freeze fresh grapes and enjoy them instead of sugary iced treats.
- Place a pack of dried fruit in your car, purse, briefcase, bookbag, or lunch box for a between-meal snack.
- Enjoy fruits and vegetables as snacks by keeping them ready to eat in the refrigerator or in a display bowl at all times.

Herbs

Use fresh and dried herbs, the leaves and stems of a wide variety of aromatic plants, to enhance many dishes.

Choose fresh herbs that look fresh and bright. Avoid items with signs of wilting or discoloration. For a final burst of flavor and color, add fresh herbs toward the end of cooking.

Grow your own herbs. A small garden plot or planter box in your kitchen window will supply you with most of the herbs you'll need for the recipes in this book.

Buy dried herbs in small quantities. Dried herbs lose their flavor over time. Purchase only what you will use in a few months. Add dried herbs in the earlier stages of cooking, crushing them first to release their concentrated flavor. When substituting dried for fresh, use about one third the amount.

Using grains, legumes, and potatoes

a s different as grains, legumes, and potatoes are, these foods share one common trait: These ingredients are the foundation of eating well. Often referred to as a meal's "starches," they are a rich source of complex carbohydrates and fiber. It is easy to eat the majority of your calories from this food group because of the plentiful choices. From breakfast cereals to whole grain lunch breads, from rice pilafs to pasta salads, from bean stews to multigrain cakes, there are dishes made from these foods available for every meal of the day. Use the guidelines that follow to enjoy more of the goodness grains, legumes, and potatoes have to offer.

Grains

Also known as cereals, grains are the widely varied seeds of grasses cultivated for food. Grain foods include rices and all wheat, oat, and rye products.

Select whole grain products as often as possible. Whole grains have not had their bran removed by milling and, as a result, are better sources of fiber.

Store all grains at room temperature. After purchase, remove all grains and grain products, such as dried pasta, from their packaging, place in tightly covered containers, and store in a darkened place. Use grain products within 1 year of purchase.

Cook grains using techniques that enhance flavor. Toasting most grains before adding them to recipes brings out their nutty flavor. Cook pasta in unsalted water just to al dente, tender but still chewy in texture. Steam rice without butter to receive the benefits of the grain without added fat. For extra body, add whole grains such as cooked brown rice or whole wheat (wholemeal) bread crumbs to ground meat or poultry.

BAKING is an ancient method that perfectly fits today's techniques for eating well because it cooks food without adding fat. Here, Whole Wheat Biscuits (recipe on page 228) fresh from the oven show how the dry heat cooks a traditional bread made better by the use of a whole grain. Baking is similar to roasting, but usually you bake items at a lower oven temperature for less time than when roasting.

ROASTING an array of potatoes in a pan in the oven sweetens and intensifies their taste. Shown here are russet, red, and Yukon gold potatoes. Just scrub the potatoes well and cover with a very light coating of nonstick cooking spray or olive oil, then sprinkle with some chopped fresh herbs or a dash of ground spices before placing them in the oven. Use this technique for a variety of vegetables.

Legumes

The term "legumes" refers to a large family of plants whose seeds develop inside pods and are usually dried for ease of storage, including beans, lentils, and peas.

Expand your legume options. All supermarkets carry a selection of common legumes, usually including white or navy beans, lima beans, pinto and black beans, black-eyed peas, split peas, and brown lentils. Shop in ethnic markets for less common legumes. Indian markets, for example, usually offer a good selection of lentils, including pink and orange-colored ones. Chickpeas are readily found in Italian delicatessens, where they are more likely to be labeled "garbanzo beans." Buying legumes in bulk often provides the freshest product at the greatest savings.

Purchase legumes recently dried. Whether buying bulk or packaged legumes, get them from a source with a quick turnover. Newer product cooks more quickly.

Look for legumes of a uniform size that will cook evenly. Whatever you buy and where ever you find them, look for those legumes free of mold or any other impurities.

Store legumes at room temperature. After purchase, place in tightly covered jars away from heat, light, and moisture. They will keep well for up to 1 year.

Carefully sort legumes before use. All legumes may include a few small stones or fibers that you need to remove, along with any misshapen or discolored items, before cooking.

Presoak large dried legumes before cooking. Beans and other large dried legumes such as chickpeas and black-eyed peas require presoaking, a step that rehydrates them for more even cooking. Once soaked, the beans are ready to cook. Split peas and lentils require no presoaking.

For convenience, use canned legumes. Already prepared legumes are fine in dishes that don't require long simmering. Rinse them well, though, to eliminate the salt that may have been added during processing. Or, if you like, precook your own dried legumes in quantity, then portion them into individual labeled and dated freezer containers, and use within 1 year.

Potatoes

Potatoes are the thick, tuberous roots of a kind of vine. The wide variety of potatoes can be divided into a few basic categories, called for in specific recipes in this book. In most cases, various types of potatoes are interchangeable in recipes. From a culinary standpoint, potatoes are grouped with grains and legumes. From

---

enjoying more grains, legumes, and potatoes

Consider these ways to incorporate grains, legumes, and potatoes into every meal every day.

- Enjoy breakfasts that include high-fiber cereals such as bran flakes or shredded wheat.
- Substitute whole wheat (wholemeal) toast or bagels and multi-grain muffins for pastry treats.
- Make sandwiches with whole grain breads or rolls.
- Expand your grain repertoire with whole grain complements such as kasha, brown rice, wild rice, wheat berries, or tortillas.
- Snack on whole grain treats such as air-popped popcorn, baked tortillas, brown rice cakes, or whole grain flat bread (recipe on page 231).
- Feature beans, rice, pasta, or potatoes in soups, stews, casseroles, and salads.
- Use cooked or shredded raw potato in any of the ways suggested on page 23 for eating more vegetables.
- Try tofu (soybean curd) in place of meat in stir-fries.
- Use puréed beans as the basis for dips and spreads.

a nutritional standpoint, they are a starchy vegetable and count toward your daily food goal for vegetables.

Choose firm potatoes. Look for items that are nicely shaped and free of bruises or blemishes. Think sweet potato, too. Not a true potato, though resembling it in form, this tuberous vegetable has light to deep red skin and pale yellow to orange flesh.

Avoid green spots or sprouting eyes. Potatoes naturally contain small amounts of solanine, a substance that is toxic when eaten in large amounts. Solanine level is higher in potatoes that are green-tinged, wrinkled, soft, or have sprouting eyes. Although you have to eat a large quantity of green potatoes to get an upset stomach from the solanine, a little bit will taste unpleasantly bitter.

Store potatoes, unwashed, in a dark place. Short storage time and protection from light helps prevent the development of solanine. Keep at a cool room temperature between 45 and 50°F (8 and 10°C). Do not wrap potatoes in plastic bags, which trap moisture. Instead, leave them unwrapped or wrap loosely in brown paper. Use potatoes within 10 days of purchase.

Scrub potatoes before cooking. Wash potatoes under cold running water to remove any dirt. Trim away any green spots you may have missed when shopping. If possible, cook and eat potatoes with their peels, to enjoy maximum nutrients and fiber.

Using poultry, seafood, and meat

*O*nce you begin to think about and use them in a new way, poultry, seafood, and lean meats can be a part of eating well. The first step is to enjoy more meals without them. When you do serve these foods, use smaller amounts in more creative ways. Rather than placing poultry, seafood, and meat center-stage at meals, think of them as garnishes to vegetables, fruits, grains, and legumes. Eat no more than three servings daily. One serving is 2 to 3 ounces (60 to 90 grams), an amount equivalent in size to a deck of cards. Delicious and satisfying recipes that use recommended serving amounts of animal products begin on page 178.

traditional pairings

An elegant winter meal is a perfect opportunity to impress guests with the joys of eating well. A small lamb chop served over white beans is well within the food goals for meat servings. After a flavorful carrot soup starter, serve the entree with a spinach complement. Finish the meal with a tropical fruit dessert (above). The great taste belies the menu's attributes of just 840 calories (3,516 kilojoules) and only 21 percent calories from fat. For a complete recipe list and nutritional analysis of the Winter Menu, see page 19.

Poultry

The poultry recipes in this book feature chicken and turkey. Consider other types of poultry as well, including game birds, realizing that these are usually higher in fat.

Choose lean cuts. The leanest poultry choice is white meat from the breast of chicken or turkey, without the skin. Skinless dark meat has almost twice the fat calories as white meat. Most stores carry both ground chicken and turkey in different qualities. Look for packages of ground breast meat. It has less fat than a package of mixed ground poultry that may contain the skin. Select poultry that looks moist and supple. Avoid poultry with signs of drying, discoloration, blemishes, or bruising. Fresh poultry has a good, clean scent, free of odors.

Use fresh poultry within 2 days. Store poultry loosely wrapped in the coldest part of your refrigerator. To freeze fresh poultry, wrap it in airtight freezer bags; store for up to 6 months. Thaw frozen poultry in the refrigerator before use. Bacteria can grow rapidly on poultry at room temperature.

Avoid poultry contamination of other foods. Before cooking, rinse and pat dry all poultry pieces. Wash your hands and all utensils and surfaces that come into contact with raw poultry or its juices before using them for other foods.

Cook poultry thoroughly before eating. To test poultry pieces for doneness, cut into the thickest part to see if the meat is cooked through to its center. Any juices should run clear. The meat should show no signs of uncooked pink flesh.

Seafood

For the purposes of meal planning, the word "seafood" includes all fish and shellfish from the sea—as well as freshwater fish.

Seek out a seafood source on which you can rely. Whether it's a supermarket or a specialty fish market, a reputable seafood retailer carries a variety of quality fish and shellfish items. Avoid "fishy" smelling seafood. The surface of good seafood will look moist, bright, and lustrous; smell clean; and be free of any dry spots and discoloration. Whole fish at their freshest have bright, clear eyes; shiny, well-attached scales; bright pink or red gills; and firm, springy flesh. If only frozen fish is available, buy it still frozen rather than defrosted.

Keep seafood cold. Securely wrap fresh fish and shellfish in a plastic bag or moisture-proof paper in the coldest part of your refrigerator. Use fresh fish within 2 days, and preferably 1 day, of purchase. Store frozen seafood up to 6 months for lean varieties and 3 months for fattier fish such as salmon or tuna. Defrost frozen seafood in the refrigerator just before cooking. Cook frozen fish within 1 day of defrosting.

Take care not to overcook fish. As a general rule, allow 10 minutes of cooking time for every 1 inch (2.5 cm) of thickness for medium. To test for doneness, use the tip of a small, sharp knife to cut into the flesh, which, while still appearing moist, should separate into flakes and be opaque throughout (except for salmon and tuna, which may be cooked medium-rare).

Meat

An added benefit to using less beef, pork, and lamb is that you may afford to purchase better cuts, which often have less fat.

Avoid meat that is heavily marbled. Marbled meat is veined with fat. Look for moistness and bright color. Pink meat is a sign of freshness, although vacuum-packed meats may look slightly purplish for lack of exposure to air. Check labels on ground meat. Most stores carry several qualities of ground beef, with varying percentages of fat by weight. Look for packages with the lowest percentage.

Keep meat cold. Keep meat loosely wrapped in its store packaging in the coldest part of your refrigerator. Use whole cuts within 3 to 4 days and ground meat within 2 days of purchase. Freeze meat in store packaging. Leave on the wrapping and add a second layer of airtight, freezerproof plastic before placing in the freezer.

Thaw frozen meat in the refrigerator. Do not refreeze meat that has been defrosted. Cook previously frozen meat within 1 to 2 days of defrosting.

Trim away all visible fat before cooking. If not trimmed away by the butcher, use a sharp knife to remove all the fat you can see. Rinse and pat dry whole cuts of meat before cooking. Dispose of meat wrappings.

Extend smaller meat servings. Cut meat into small pieces before using in recipes. Add moisture and body to ground meat and extend small quantities by combining it with shredded raw or cooked puréed vegetables, bread crumbs, or cooked rice.

Cook meat thoroughly. To test for doneness, check thin cuts or small pieces simply by cutting into a sample. You can safely eat beef or lamb medium-rare, which looks reddish-pink in the center, or it may be cooked longer, if you like. Cook ground beef medium to well done. Cook pork to medium-well, still moist but with just a hint of pinkness.

Cooking techniques for eating well

*U*sing cooking techniques that highlight the inherent tastes, textures, aromas, and colors of foods, you can transform common ingredients into uncommonly delicious meals. There is nothing particularly difficult, unusual, or complicated about cooking techniques for eating well. The simple methods described here are standard practices used by experienced cooks. These cooking techniques demonstrate how you can best capture the flavor and nutrients from your food without adding tremendous amounts of fat or salt. Once you've mastered these techniques, use them in the recipes throughout this book as well as when you cook your favorite dishes.

Baking

Of course, baking refers to cooking breads and desserts. The same method can be used to cook uniform-sized pieces of vegetables, fruit, seafood, poultry, or lean meat in an open pan or dish surrounded by the hot, dry air of an oven. Baking is a cooking method that generally adds no fat to a dish.

Braising

Braising slowly cooks small pieces of food with a small quantity of liquid in an open or covered pan on top of the stove or in the oven. In some recipes, the cooking liquid is reduced after the initial cooking to form a flavorful, nutrient-rich sauce.

Enhancing

There are many clever ways to enhance a food's flavor without adding fat, salt, or sugar. Use herbs, both fresh and dried, and spices to contribute bright color, vivid taste, and wonderful aroma. Citrus zests add a spark of flavor and color. A dash of flavorful vinegar, a sprinkling of toasted nuts or seeds, or a garnish of bell peppers (capsicums) are other interesting enhancements.

POACHING is a technique in which you cook a variety of foods in a liquid medium that becomes part of the dish. Use it for ingredients that contain little inherent fat, as all of it ends up in the sauce. Here, tomato juice, wine, and vinegar are used for stovetop-poaching in Sweet Potato and Shrimp Gumbo (recipe on page 203).

STEAMING is a practically foolproof way to cook almost any vegetable. You can get excellent results using an inexpensive metal basket in a cooking pot with a snug lid. Serve steamed vegetables like this mix of broccoli, carrots, and cauliflower on their own, combine them with a grain, or use them to top a pasta.

Grilling and Broiling

Both of these time-honored cooking methods expose fairly thin pieces of food to direct heat. To grill outdoors, place the food on a grill rack above a bed of charcoal embers or gas-heated rocks. For grilling smaller items, use a long-handled grill basket, which prevents pieces from slipping through the rack. To broil, place food on a broiler rack below a heat element. Both methods allow fat to drip away from the food.

Poaching

To poach foods, gently simmer ingredients in water or a flavorful liquid such as broth, vinegar, or juice until they are cooked through and tender. For stovetop poaching, choose a covered pan that best fits the size and shape of the foods, so you use a minimum amount of liquid. You can also poach foods in foil packets in the oven (recipe on page 215).

Roasting

Like baking, only usually at a higher temperature, roasting uses the dry heat of an oven to slowly cook larger pieces of food. You can roast foods on a baking sheet or in a roasting pan. For poultry, seafood, and meat, place a rack inside the roasting pan so that the fat in the ingredients can drip away during cooking.

Sautéing

Sautéing rapidly cooks relatively small or thin pieces of food. If you choose a good-quality nonstick pan, you can cook food with the addition of little or no fat. Depending on the recipe, use broths, nonstick cooking spray, or water in place of oil.

Steaming

One of the simplest cooking techniques to master is steaming food in a perforated basket suspended above simmering liquid. If you use a flavorful liquid or add enhancement to the water, you'll flavor the food as it cooks.

Stir-Frying

A traditional Asian method, stir-frying quickly cooks small, uniform-sized pieces of food while they are rapidly stirred in a hemispherical nonstick wok or large nonstick frying pan. You need only a small amount of oil or nonstick cooking spray. For more details on stir-frying, see page 68.

keeping a safe and clean kitchen

All foods naturally contain small amounts of bacteria. When food is poorly handled, improperly cooked, or inadequately stored, these bacteria can multiply in great enough numbers to cause illness. To protect yourself:

Shop smart. Don't buy food in cans or jars with dents or bulging lids. Choose perishable foods last and refrigerate them as soon as possible after purchase.

Wash your hands. Clean with warm soapy water before and after handling ingredients, particularly raw poultry, seafood, and meat, and before emptying the dishwasher, setting the table, and eating.

Use clean tools. After use, wash all implements thoroughly with warm soapy water, put them through a dishwasher, or use a commercial antibacterial treatment. Wash tools or platters that have touched raw animal foods before using them again.

Keep towels clean. Change kitchen towels every day, and more often when household members are sick. Every few days, run sponges and scrubbers through the dishwasher or boil or microwave them for 2 minutes to keep bacteria at bay.

Rinse produce and raw animal foods. Before cooking, thoroughly rinse or peel fruits and vegetables. Rinse pieces of poultry, meats, and seafood in cold running water, including the body cavities of poultry.

Clean up spills quickly. While there is no need to cry over spilt milk, it is important to clean up all spills quickly to prevent bacterial growth.

Keep cutting boards clean and separate. Always use separate cutting boards for animal foods and produce, to avoid cross-contamination. After use, wash cutting boards thoroughly with warm, soapy water. Sterilize the boards periodically, either by washing in the dishwasher at the hottest setting or by hand-washing and then rinsing in a solution of 4 cups (32 fl oz/1 l) warm water and 1 teaspoon bleach. Use the same solution regularly to sterilize kitchen counters and other work surfaces.

Marinate foods for minimum times. Marinate raw foods at room temperature for no longer than 30 minutes. When marinating foods in the refrigerator, keep them covered and marinate for no longer than 1 hour.

Store foods carefully. Check expiration dates on packaged items. Refrigerate leftovers or freeze in a tightly covered container immediately or within 2 hours of serving.

give all your meals a nutritious beginning with appetizers, salads, and soups based on fresh vegetables and fruits. The common goal of the wide variety of recipes in this chapter is to excite your appetite while adhering to the basics of eating well. Starter recipes are versatile: Use the recipes in this chapter for traditional first courses or combine several of the starter recipes to compose complete meals. Simply double or triple these appetizer recipes to create a party buffet. Colorful and crunchy vegetable salads and delicious fruit combinations contribute a vast assortment of nutrients without adding large amounts of calories, cholesterol, or fats. Dressings made from flavored vinegars, herbs, and fruit juices allow the wonderful nature of both vegetables and fruits to shine through without being weighed down by heavy creams and oils. Soup is another creative way to eat more vegetables. All of these appetizers, salads, and soups will get you off to a good start at eating well.

starters

Roasted red potatoes with Chive sauce

This versatile potato dish makes a fabulous first course for a multi-course meal. It is also a wonderful party appetizer. The yogurt dressing, a delicious alternative to cream dressing, is good with a variety of raw vegetables as well. If you find very small potatoes, cook them whole.

SERVES: 6 | **PREPARATION:** 10 minutes | **COOKING:** 45 minutes

2 lb (1 kg) red-skinned potatoes

2 teaspoons olive oil

1 tablespoon dried rosemary

1/2 teaspoon ground pepper

Chive Sauce (recipe follows)

♦ Preheat an oven to 425°F (220°C). Coat a heavy baking dish or a medium cast-iron frying pan with nonstick cooking spray.

♦ Using a fork, prick each potato a few times. Halve any that are more than 1¹/₂ inches (4 cm) across.

♦ In a large bowl, combine the potatoes, olive oil, rosemary, and pepper. Toss to coat the potatoes evenly with the seasonings. Transfer the potatoes to the prepared baking dish, spreading them in a single layer.

♦ Bake, stirring once halfway through the cooking time, until the potatoes are tender, 40–45 minutes.

♦ To serve, place the potatoes in a large bowl. Serve with the sauce.

Chive sauce

MAKES: 1¹/₄ cups (10 fl oz/310 ml) | **PREPARATION:** 2 minutes

1¹/₄ cups (10 oz/315 g) plain nonfat yogurt

1/4 cup (1/2 oz/15 g) chopped fresh chives

2 drops hot pepper sauce

1/4 teaspoon salt

♦ In a small bowl, stir together the yogurt, chives, hot pepper sauce, and salt. Serve now, or refrigerate in a tightly covered container for up to 2 days.

Garlic and bean purée on pitas

Roasting a whole head of garlic brings out the inherent sweetness in this pungent member of the onion family. In this Middle Eastern–inspired party platter, roasted garlic is blended with beans to form a smooth dip for vegetables and pita, the bread staple of the region.

SERVES: 8 | **PREPARATION:** 25 minutes | **COOKING:** 1 hour

1 garlic head

2 teaspoons plus 1 tablespoon olive oil

3 cups (21 oz/655 g) cooked white beans (see page 160) or canned white beans, rinsed and drained

1/3 cup (3 oz/90 g) plain nonfat yogurt

3 tablespoons chopped fresh chives

1/2 teaspoon ground pepper

4 whole wheat (wholemeal) pita breads

1/2 teaspoon dried oregano

2 bell peppers (capsicums), halved, stemmed, seeded, and cut into strips

12 celery stalks, halved

◆ Preheat an oven to 325°F (165°C).

◆ Using a sharp knife, slice off the top 1/2 inch (12 mm) of the garlic head. Discard any loose papery skin covering the head, taking care to keep the cloves intact. Rub 1 teaspoon of the olive oil on the garlic head. Place the head in a small roasting pan and cover with aluminum foil.

◆ Bake until the garlic feels soft when squeezed gently, 40–45 minutes. Cool completely. To remove the garlic from the skins, using your fingers, pinch the pulp from the cloves.

◆ In a blender or food processor, combine the garlic, 1 tablespoon of the olive oil, beans, yogurt, chives, and pepper. Process until blended. You will have about 3 cups (24 fl oz/750 ml) bean purée. Serve now, or refrigerate in a tightly covered container for up to 3 days.

◆ To make the pitas, preheat an oven to 400°F (200°C).

◆ Using a fork, prick each pita several times. Rub one side of each pita with the remaining 1 teaspoon olive oil, then sprinkle with the oregano. Cut each pita into 8 triangles and place, seasoned side up, on a baking sheet.

◆ Bake until crisp and browned, about 12 minutes. Serve now, or store in a tightly covered container at room temperature for up to 3 days.

◆ To serve, place the bean purée in the center of a large platter. Surround with the pita triangles, pepper strips, and celery for dipping.

PER SERVING

Calories	253
Kilojoules	1,059
Protein	12 g
Carbohydrates	42 g
Total Fat	5 g
Saturated Fat	<1 g
Cholesterol	0 mg
Sodium	236 mg
Dietary Fiber	6 g

Asparagus and avocado wraps

Food rolled in an edible wrapper and eaten by hand is a tradition in many cuisines, including Chinese mu shu and Mexican burritos. This ancient idea takes a modern twist in the proliferation of restaurants serving "wraps." Serve this wrap as an appetizer or for a quick lunch.

SERVES: 6 | **PREPARATION:** 15 minutes | **COOKING:** 8 minutes

24 asparagus

1 ripe avocado (8 oz/250 g), pitted and peeled

1 tablespoon lime juice

1 garlic clove, minced

1½ cups (15 oz/470 g) cooked, cold brown long-grain rice (see page 107)

3 tablespoons plain nonfat yogurt

3 whole wheat (wholemeal) tortillas, 10 inches (25 cm) in diameter

⅓ cup (½ oz/15 g) cilantro (fresh coriander) leaves

2 tablespoons chopped red (Spanish) onion

♦ In a medium saucepan over high heat, bring 2 inches (5 cm) water to a boil. Place the asparagus in a steamer basket, cover, and steam until just tender, 6–8 minutes. Remove the asparagus and immediately rinse in cold water to stop the cooking. Drain thoroughly.

♦ In a small bowl, mash the avocado, lime juice, and garlic into a coarse purée.

♦ In another small bowl, stir together the rice and yogurt to mix well.

♦ Heat a dry large frying pan (not one with a nonstick surface) over medium heat. One at a time, heat the tortillas in the hot pan until softened, about 20 seconds per side.

♦ Lay the tortillas flat on a clean work surface. Spread the avocado mixture equally among the tortillas. Top each with an equal amount of the rice mixture, asparagus, cilantro, and onion.

♦ Fold in both sides and the bottom of each tortilla up over the filling, then roll to close. If made in advance, cover with plastic wrap and refrigerate for up to 1 hour. Return to room temperature before serving.

♦ To serve, cut each wrap in half crosswise.

PER SERVING

Calories	263
Kilojoules	1,101
Protein	7 g
Carbohydrates	40 g
Total Fat	9 g
Saturated Fat	2 g
Cholesterol	<1 mg
Sodium	289 mg
Dietary Fiber	4 g

Steamed vegetables with Roasted pepper sauce

Using a greater variety of vegetables adds interest and nutrients to your menus. Replace salty snacks with this variety of vegetables and simple, flavor-packed sauce. This serves 6 as a first course or 8 as an appetizer. Purchase prepared peppers for the sauce or roast your own (see page 99).

SERVES: 6 | **PREPARATION:** 30 minutes | **COOKING:** 30 minutes

3 small artichokes, quartered

3 carrots, cut into slices

24 green beans

1 lb (500 g) broccoli, cut into florets

3 zucchini (courgettes), cut into slices

3 yellow crookneck squash, cut into slices

Roasted Pepper Sauce (recipe follows)

◆ In a large pot over high heat, bring 3 inches (7.5 cm) water to a boil. Insert the steamer basket, cover, reduce heat to medium-low, and steam the vegetables—in batches, if necessary—until just tender: artichokes, 30 minutes; carrots, 12–14 minutes; green beans, about 10 minutes; broccoli florets, 5–6 minutes; zucchini and squash, 5 minutes. Cool to the touch.

◆ To serve, mound the vegetables on a large platter. Serve with the sauce.

PER SERVING

Calories	107
Kilojoules	447
Protein	6 g
Carbohydrates	21 g
Total Fat	2 g
Saturated Fat	<1 g
Cholesterol	<1 mg
Sodium	117 mg
Dietary Fiber	8 g

Roasted pepper sauce

MAKES: 2 cups (16 fl oz/500 ml) | **PREPARATION:** 5 minutes

2 cups (12 oz/375 g) roasted (see page 99), sliced red bell peppers (capsicums)

1/4 cup (2 oz/60 g) plain nonfat yogurt

2 tablespoons red wine vinegar

2 tablespoons olive oil

1 tablespoon Dijon mustard

1/4 teaspoon ground pepper

2 tablespoons chopped fresh oregano or 1 teaspoon dried oregano

◆ In a blender or food processor, combine the peppers, yogurt, vinegar, oil, mustard, and pepper. Process until smooth. Add the oregano and process a few seconds longer. Transfer to a small bowl. Serve now, or refrigerate in a tightly covered container for up to 3 days.

PER TABLESPOON

Calories	13
Kilojoules	54
Protein	<1 g
Carbohydrates	1 g
Total Fat	<1 g
Saturated Fat	<1 g
Cholesterol	<1 mg
Sodium	33 mg
Dietary Fiber	<1 g

Choosing mushrooms

Fresh and dried mushrooms offer a lot of good taste and few calories in an unassuming little package. Mushrooms bring to savory dishes a satisfying taste and texture with virtually no fat or sodium.

You can use most mushrooms interchangeably in recipes.

White. *Also called button mushrooms, these are the most familiar fresh variety. Raw, they have a nutlike flavor; cooked, their flavor is more concentrated.*

Cremini. *A darker, firmer cousin to the whites, these hold up better when cooked.*

Portobello. *Simply white mushrooms that have grown larger and become more flavorful, portobellos are good candidates for stuffing, as in the recipe at right, and also for grilling.*

Oyster. *These mushrooms have an almost briny flavor that makes them a good choice for stir-frying and braising.*

Shiitake. *Fresh or dried, these impart a smoky flavor when cooked.*

PER SERVING

Calories	52
Kilojoules	219
Protein	2 g
Carbohydrates	6 g
Total Fat	3 g
Saturated Fat	<1 g
Cholesterol	1 mg
Sodium	70 mg
Dietary Fiber	1 g

Tarragon rice–stuffed mushrooms

Enjoy a bite, or three, of grain-filled mushrooms and start any meal in elegant style. Reduced-fat mayonnaise, even the small amount used to bind the ingredients here, at only 50 calories and 5 grams of fat per tablespoon, is a better choice than regular mayonnaise.

SERVES: 6 | **PREPARATION:** 20 minutes | **COOKING:** 15 minutes

18 white mushrooms

1/4 cup (2 fl oz/60 ml) canned nonfat reduced-sodium chicken broth

1 shallot, minced

1/2 cup (2 1/2 oz/75 g) cooked, cold long-grain white rice (see page 107)

2 teaspoons reduced-fat mayonnaise

1 teaspoon chopped fresh tarragon

2 tablespoons grated Parmesan cheese

2 teaspoons olive oil

1/4 teaspoon paprika

♦ Preheat an oven to 375°F (190°C).

♦ Remove the stems from the mushrooms and chop the stems finely.

♦ In a nonstick frying pan over medium-high heat, bring the broth to a boil. Add the shallot and mushroom stems and cook, stirring occasionally, until the vegetables are tender and most of the liquid has evaporated, about 2 minutes.

♦ In a bowl, combine the vegetable mixture, rice, mayonnaise, tarragon, and half the cheese.

♦ Using a paper towel, wipe out the frying pan and place over medium heat. Add the oil and mushroom caps and sauté until coated with oil, 20–30 seconds. Arrange the caps, stem end up, on a baking sheet. Mound about 2 teaspoons of the rice mixture in each cap. Sprinkle with the remaining cheese. If made in advance, cover with plastic wrap and refrigerate for up to 8 hours.

♦ Bake until the cheese is lightly browned and the mushrooms are tender but still hold their shape, about 10 minutes.

♦ Before serving, dust each cap lightly with the paprika.

Spicy spring greens salad

Combine different greens to add interest and texture to your salads. Butter (Boston) lettuce, one of the three greens used here, is mildly tangy and blends beautifully with the slightly tart vinaigrette. If you wash the greens and make the croutons ahead, you can put this salad together in moments.

SERVES: 6 | **PREPARATION:** 15 minutes | **COOKING:** 30 minutes

1 egg white

2 teaspoons olive oil

1 teaspoon Worcestershire sauce

1 teaspoon dried thyme

1 garlic clove, minced

1/8 teaspoon cayenne pepper

4 slices whole wheat (wholemeal) sandwich bread, cut into 1/2-inch (12-mm) cubes

1/4 cup (1 oz/30 g) walnut pieces

2 bunches watercress, 8 oz (250 g) total, stemmed

1 large head butter (Boston) lettuce

1 head Belgian endive (chicory/witloof)

1/4 teaspoon ground pepper

6 tablespoons Tarragon Vinaigrette (recipe on page 120)

♦ Preheat an oven to 325°F (165°C). Coat a large, shallow baking pan with nonstick cooking spray.

♦ In a large bowl, combine the egg white, olive oil, Worcestershire sauce, thyme, garlic, and cayenne. Add the bread cubes and walnuts and toss until the bread and nuts are evenly coated with the seasonings, about 1 minute. Spread in the prepared pan.

♦ Bake, stirring every 10 minutes, until the bread is well browned and crisp, about 30 minutes. Cool completely, then store in a tightly covered container until serving.

♦ To prepare the salad, separate the watercress into sprigs, dropping them into a large bowl. Tear the lettuce leaves into pieces and add them to the bowl. With a sharp knife, cut the endive crosswise into 3/4-inch (2-cm) pieces. Toss the pieces lightly to separate the layers, then add to the bowl. Add the pepper and vinaigrette and toss to coat the greens evenly with the dressing.

♦ To serve, divide the dressed greens among individual plates and scatter an equal amount of the crouton mixture over each salad.

cooking clinic

Washing salad greens

Take advantage of the fresh salad greens that come prewashed in sealed plastic bags in supermarket produce sections. As you begin to expand your repertoire of salad ingredients, however, you'll come to rely on the wide array of greens that need to be washed.

You can simply rinse most leaves with cold water. The easiest way is to run the tap in your kitchen sink and hold a few leaves at a time under the stream of water. If you are conservation-minded, however, you can partly fill a sink with water and add the leaves. Swish them around with your hands, then lift from the water and drain.

When washing leaves such as spinach or kale, it may take several changes of water to rid them of all the grit.

Make sure all greens are dry before using so that the dressing will not get watered down. Pat dry using a clean kitchen towel or spin in a salad spinner.

PER SERVING

Calories	171
Kilojoules	715
Protein	5 g
Carbohydrates	19 g
Total Fat	9 g
Saturated Fat	1 g
Cholesterol	0 mg
Sodium	304 mg
Dietary Fiber	3 g

A splash of vinegar can add vibrant flavor to a savory dish without a hint of fat or sodium and almost no calories. Try vinegar not only in its familiar role as part of a salad dressing, but also as a condiment for soups, sprinkled over steamed vegetables, or added to marinades.

Wine vinegars. *These reflect the characteristics of the white, red, or rosé wines or champagne from which they were made, so select a good-quality brand.*

Balsamic vinegar. *Not, strictly speaking, a wine vinegar, although it is classed among them. Intense and complex in flavor, this specialty of Modena, Italy, is reduced grape juice that has been aged in wood.*

Other vinegars. *Cider vinegar retains the wonderful character of apples. Rice wine is a clean-tasting, brisk condiment favored in Asian kitchens. Golden-colored malt vinegar is distilled from soured beer and has a wonderfully rich, almost woodsy flavor.*

Store vinegars in their original bottles, tightly capped, in a cool, dark place.

PER SERVING

Calories	63
Kilojoules	263
Protein	2 g
Carbohydrates	15 g
Total Fat	<1 g
Saturated Fat	<1 g
Cholesterol	0 mg
Sodium	64 mg
Dietary Fiber	3 g

Herbed carrot and beet salad

This bright combination benefits from being made ahead, which gives the flavors time to marry; so consider it the next time you're asked to bring a dish to a party. Not only will you be sharing a feast of flavors, you'll also be providing a lower-calorie, lower-sodium, nonfat, and vitamin-filled starter.

SERVES: 6 | **PREPARATION:** 10 minutes | **CHILLING:** 60 minutes

8 carrots, peeled and shredded

3 beets, peeled and shredded

2 garlic cloves, minced

1/3 cup (1/2 oz/15 g) coarsely chopped cilantro (fresh coriander)

1/3 cup (3 fl oz/80 ml) rice vinegar

♦ In a bowl, combine the carrots, beets, garlic, and cilantro. Add the rice vinegar and toss to mix well. Cover and refrigerate for at least 1 hour to allow the flavors to marry.

♦ To serve, toss well and divide among individual plates.

Spinach salad with Raspberry vinaigrette

Spinach salad, served here with round versions of Whole Wheat Biscuits (recipe on page 228), gains a sensational flavor from a fine, fruity dressing. Pectin, often used to give body to jams and jellies, helps to thicken the vinaigrette without the fat that lots of oil would add.

SERVES: 8 | **PREPARATION:** 20 minutes

Raspberry Vinaigrette
  (recipe follows)

2 lb (1 kg) spinach, stemmed

1/2 cup (2 oz/60 g) thinly
  sliced red (Spanish) onion

1/4 teaspoon ground pepper

1/4 cup (1 oz/30 g) sunflower
  seeds, toasted (see page 127)

◆ In a large bowl, combine the vinaigrette, spinach, onion, pepper, and half the sunflower seeds. Toss to coat the spinach with the dressing.

◆ To serve, divide among individual plates. Top each with an equal amount of the remaining sunflower seeds.

PER SERVING

Calories	100
Kilojoules	419
Protein	3 g
Carbohydrates	11 g
Total Fat	5 g
Saturated Fat	<1 g
Cholesterol	0 mg
Sodium	103 mg
Dietary Fiber	2 g

Raspberry vinaigrette

MAKES: 1/2 cup (4 fl oz/125 ml) | **PREPARATION:** 2 minutes | **CHILLING:** 60 minutes

1/3 cup (3 fl oz/80 ml) thawed
  unsweetened apple juice
  concentrate

3 tablespoons raspberry vinegar

3 tablespoons water

2 tablespoons powdered fruit
  pectin

2 tablespoons olive oil

2 teaspoons Dijon mustard

1 tablespoon chopped fresh
  thyme or 1/2 teaspoon
  dried thyme

1/4 teaspoon ground pepper

◆ In a small bowl, combine the apple juice, vinegar, water, and pectin. Whisk until the pectin dissolves, about 1 minute. Add the olive oil, mustard, thyme, and pepper and whisk until blended.

◆ Refrigerate for at least 1 hour before using; the pectin will cause the dressing to thicken slightly as it chills.

PER TABLESPOON

Calories	59
Kilojoules	247
Protein	<1 g
Carbohydrates	7 g
Total Fat	3 g
Saturated Fat	<1 g
Cholesterol	0 mg
Sodium	38 mg
Dietary Fiber	<1 g

Autumn fruit salad

While summer produce cries out to be used in salads, don't forget the sweet jewels of autumn. Apple juice concentrate is used throughout this book to replace oil, both as a base for salad dressings, as here, and as a cooking medium. Look for unsweetened versions and do not dilute before using.

SERVES: 6 | **PREPARATION:** 20 minutes

2/3 cup (5 fl oz/160 ml) thawed unsweetened apple juice concentrate

3 tablespoons lime juice

1 tablespoon Dijon mustard

1 teaspoon ground cumin

3 heads butter (Boston) lettuce, 1 lb (500 g) total, torn into leaves

3 navel oranges

3 red-skinned apples

8 dried Mission or Calimyrna figs, cut into quarters

3 tablespoons pumpkin seeds, toasted (see page 127)

♦ In a small bowl, whisk together the apple juice concentrate, lime juice, mustard, and cumin until blended.

♦ Divide the lettuce leaves equally among 6 salad plates.

♦ Peel the oranges and remove the white pith. Cut the oranges crosswise into 1/4-inch-thick (6-mm) slices. Arrange the orange slices, overlapping slightly, on the lettuce leaves.

♦ Cut the apples in half lengthwise. Using a melon baller or a grapefruit spoon, remove the core and seeds from each half. Cut each half lengthwise into thin wedges. Arrange over the lettuce leaves, fanning the slices slightly.

♦ To serve, drizzle 2 tablespoons of the dressing over each salad. Top each with an equal amount of the figs and pumpkin seeds.

Pear and pomegranate salad

This stunning autumn starter could be called a potassium salad, as pomegranates are rich in this essential mineral. Pomegranates are refreshing and beautiful, though they can be messy to seed. Take care when preparing this, as the crimson pomegranate juice can stain.

SERVES: 6 | **PREPARATION:** 15 minutes | **CHILLING:** 30 minutes

1 pomegranate

6 green-skinned pears, 2¹/₂ lb (1.25 kg) total

3 tablespoons lime juice

2 tablespoons minced fresh tarragon

♦ Using a knife, slit the pomegranate several times, then pull it apart into rough chunks. Pry out the clusters of red seeds. Discard the membrane.

♦ Halve and core the pears, then cut them into bite-sized pieces.

♦ In a large bowl, stir together the pears and lime juice. Add the tarragon and pomegranate seeds and toss gently to combine. Cover and refrigerate for at least 30 minutes to allow the flavors to marry.

♦ To serve, divide among individual plates.

PER SERVING

Calories	123
Kilojoules	514
Protein	1 g
Carbohydrates	31 g
Total Fat	<1 g
Saturated Fat	<1 g
Cholesterol	0 mg
Sodium	2 mg
Dietary Fiber	4 g

Minted Mediterranean fruit mix

In winter, citrus is at its seasonal peak and is a perfect choice for fruit salads. In addition, citrus is one of your best sources of the antioxidant vitamin C. Fresh mint adds zing to this colorful combination. If you want a nonfat version of this recipe, eliminate the walnut oil and olives.

SERVES: 6 | **PREPARATION:** 20 minutes

2 large Ruby Red grapefruits

3 large navel oranges

1 cup (1 oz/30 g) fresh mint leaves

¹/₄ cup (1 oz/30 g) kalamata olives, pitted and sliced

1 tablespoon walnut oil

¹/₄ teaspoon ground pepper

6 curly endive (chicory/witloof) leaves

♦ Working over a sieve set in a large bowl, peel and segment the grapefruits and oranges. Remove and discard any seeds.

♦ Pour off all but 2 tablespoons of the juice from the bowl, reserving it for another use. To the 2 tablespoons juice, add the grapefruit and orange segments, mint, olives, oil, and pepper. Toss gently to combine.

♦ To serve, arrange the curly endive leaves on individual plates. Top each with an equal amount of the fruit.

PER SERVING

Calories	110
Kilojoules	460
Protein	2 g
Carbohydrates	20 g
Total Fat	4 g
Saturated Fat	<1 g
Cholesterol	0 mg
Sodium	94 mg
Dietary Fiber	3 g

Curried potato, leek, and apple soup

The spice blend curry powder imparts a classic taste of India to this hearty soup. Tart-sweet apples add a fruity complexity that balances the mild onion flavor of the leeks. If you don't have an apple, 1 cup (9 oz/280 g) of unsweetened applesauce will do.

SERVES: 6 | **PREPARATION:** 20 minutes | **COOKING:** 20 minutes

1³/₄ cups (14 fl oz/430 ml) canned vegetable broth

5 cups (40 fl oz/1.25 l) water

3 large russet potatoes, peeled and coarsely chopped

3 leeks, white part only, thinly sliced

1 tart green apple such as Granny Smith, peeled, cored, and chopped

2 teaspoons curry powder

2 teaspoons lemon juice

¹/₂ teaspoon ground cumin

3 tablespoons chopped fresh flat-leaf (Italian) parsley

♦ In a pan over high heat, bring the broth, water, potatoes, leeks, apple, curry powder, lemon juice, and cumin to a boil.

♦ Reduce heat to medium-low, partially cover, and cook until the vegetables are very tender, about 20 minutes.

♦ Transfer the soup—in batches, if necessary—to a blender or food processor and process until smooth. Reheat as needed.

♦ To serve, ladle into individual bowls. Top each with an equal amount of the parsley.

PER SERVING

Calories	139
Kilojoules	580
Protein	3 g
Carbohydrates	31 g
Total Fat	<1 g
Saturated Fat	<1 g
Cholesterol	0 mg
Sodium	311 mg
Dietary Fiber	3 g

Dilled borscht

An old Russian saying goes, "There are as many ways to cook borscht as there are cooks." In this rustic version, beets are enhanced with lemon juice, which highlights their natural sweetness. Experiment with different colored beets for visual variety.

SERVES: 6 | **PREPARATION:** 25 minutes + 4 hours if chilling | **COOKING:** 25 minutes

6 beets, peeled and diced

3 carrots, coarsely grated

1 white onion, chopped

3 cups (9 oz/280 g) shredded cabbage

1³/₄ cups (14 fl oz/430 ml) canned vegetable broth

5 cups (40 fl oz/1.25 l) water, plus more if needed

1/2 teaspoon ground pepper

3 tablespoons lemon juice

6 tablespoons (3 fl oz/90 ml) lowfat sour cream

1/3 cup (1/3 oz/10 g) chopped fresh dill

◆ In a large saucepan, bring the beets, carrots, onion, cabbage, broth, water, and pepper to a boil.

◆ Reduce heat to low, cover, and simmer until the beets are tender, 20–25 minutes. If the soup seems too thick, stir in 1/4 cup (2 fl oz/60 ml) additional water.

◆ Remove from heat and stir in the lemon juice.

◆ To serve hot, ladle into individual bowls. Top each with 1 tablespoon of the sour cream and sprinkle with the dill.

◆ To serve cold, cool to room temperature, then cover and refrigerate until thoroughly chilled, at least 4 hours or up to 3 days. Ladle into cups and top with the sour cream and dill.

nutrition note

Beets

Folk wisdom once held that beets helped to strengthen the blood. While these root vegetables do contain some iron, the amount is small. Beets are an excellent source of potassium and contain some folic acid (folate).

Beet greens are also edible. Compared to beets, the greens contain higher levels of beta carotene and calcium.

PER SERVING

Calories	95
Kilojoules	397
Protein	3 g
Carbohydrates	19 g
Total Fat	2 g
Saturated Fat	<1 g
Cholesterol	5 mg
Sodium	400 mg
Dietary Fiber	3 g

Lentil soup with Green herb sauce

Lentils are the nutritious base for this multivegetable soup. The brightly colored Green Herb Sauce, used as a topping, is an herb pesto that substitutes tofu for the oil used in traditional recipes. Try it as a pasta sauce or use it as a spread on toast.

SERVES: 6 | **PREPARATION:** 15 minutes | **COOKING:** 45 minutes

PER SERVING

Calories	220
Kilojoules	919
Protein	16 g
Carbohydrates	33 g
Total Fat	3 g
Saturated Fat	1 g
Cholesterol	4 mg
Sodium	542 mg
Dietary Fiber	7 g

1¼ cups (9 oz/280 g) dried lentils

3 cups (24 fl oz/750 ml) water, plus more if needed

2 cups (16 fl oz/500 ml) canned vegetable broth

2 carrots, chopped

1 onion, chopped

1 celery stalk, chopped

½ cup (4 oz/125 g) Fresh Tomato Salsa (recipe on page 99)

Green Herb Sauce (recipe follows)

♦ Pick over the lentils and remove and discard any damaged ones and debris. Place in a strainer and rinse under cold running water, then drain thoroughly.

♦ In a large saucepan over high heat, bring the lentils, water, broth, carrots, onion, celery, and salsa to a boil.

♦ Reduce heat to low, cover, and simmer, stirring every 10 minutes, until the lentils are tender and the soup is thick, about 40 minutes. If the soup seems too thick, stir in ¼ cup (2 fl oz/60 ml) additional water.

♦ To serve, ladle into individual bowls. Top each with an equal amount of the herb sauce.

Green herb sauce

MAKES: 1 cup (8 fl oz/250 ml) | **PREPARATION:** 5 minutes

PER TABLESPOON

Calories	15
Kilojoules	63
Protein	1 g
Carbohydrates	1 g
Total Fat	<1 g
Saturated Fat	<1 g
Cholesterol	1 mg
Sodium	70 mg
Dietary Fiber	<1 g

1 cup (1 oz/30 g) chopped fresh flat-leaf (Italian) parsley or basil

⅔ cup (6 oz/185 g) soft (silken) tofu

⅓ cup (½ oz/15 g) coarsely chopped fresh chives or 2 teaspoons dried chives

2 garlic cloves, coarsely chopped

¼ cup (1 oz/30 g) grated Parmesan cheese

¼ teaspoon salt

♦ In a blender or food processor, combine the parsley or basil, tofu, chives, garlic, cheese, and salt. Process, stopping once or twice to scrape down the sides of the container, until the sauce is smooth and pale green, about 1 minute. Serve within 1 hour or refrigerate in a tightly covered container for up to 2 days.

Chicken and orzo soup

Orzo, a barley-shaped pasta, contributes texture to this simple soup, shown here with Multigrain Quick Bread (recipe on page 239). To gain control of sodium levels—and perhaps increase the flavor—replace the canned broth with homemade chicken stock.

SERVES: 6 | **PREPARATION:** 20 minutes | **COOKING:** 10 minutes

3½ cups (28 fl oz/875 ml) canned nonfat reduced-sodium chicken broth

5 cups (40 fl oz/1.25 l) water

8 oz (250 g) orzo

4 oz (125 g) skinless, boneless chicken breast meat, cut into bite-sized pieces

4 carrots, shredded

2 green (spring) onions, thinly sliced, including green portions

2 tablespoons coarsely chopped cilantro (fresh coriander)

1 tablespoon grated fresh ginger

½ teaspoon white wine vinegar

♦ In a large saucepan over high heat, bring the broth and water to a boil. Add the orzo and cook just until tender, about 6 minutes.

♦ Reduce heat to medium-low. Add the chicken, carrots, green onions, cilantro, ginger, and vinegar. Cook, stirring occasionally, until the chicken is opaque throughout and the vegetables are tender but still firm, about 4 minutes.

♦ To serve, ladle into individual bowls.

cooking clinic

Skimming the soup

All soups, along with any other dishes such as stews or braises that cook by simmering ingredients in a liquid, benefit from the extra, but simple, task of skimming. Skimming is necessary to remove natural albuminous substances that coagulate in the early stages of simmering and rise to the surface, forming a froth. If not removed, that froth, although harmless, can get swept back into the liquid, marring its clarity and slightly muddying its taste.

Skimming off the froth is easy; just keep a large metal spoon close at hand. As the liquid approaches a simmer and the froth begins to rise, simply draw the edge of the spoon across the surface to lift the froth away.

PER SERVING

Calories	193
Kilojoules	807
Protein	12 g
Carbohydrates	34 g
Total Fat	1 g
Saturated Fat	<1 g
Cholesterol	11 mg
Sodium	360 mg
Dietary Fiber	3 g

Sun-dried tomatoes

Drying in the hot sun is a time-honored Italian method for preserving tomatoes. It gives them a wonderfully intense flavor, a brick-red color, and a chewy consistency comparable to that of dried fruit. Commercial production is more likely to dry the tomatoes in kilns or dehydrators than with natural light.

When sun-dried tomatoes first became a popular pantry food, you could find them only in the traditional Italian form, packed into jars filled with olive oil. That made them fairly high in fat, even after the tomatoes were drained. Fortunately, now you can also find them packed dry in cellophane bags.

Unlike their oil-packed kin, dry-packed sun-dried tomatoes must be reconstituted before use. Put them in a bowl and add boiling water to cover. Leave to soak until soft and pliable, about 5 minutes, then drain.

PER SERVING

Calories	146
Kilojoules	609
Protein	5 g
Carbohydrates	31 g
Total Fat	<1 g
Saturated Fat	<1 g
Cholesterol	<1 mg
Sodium	278 mg
Dietary Fiber	3 g

Zucchini soup

You could call this "any squash soup" as you can substitute any other seasonal squash for the zucchini in this simple recipe. For a lovely light meal, serve the soup, as shown here, with Spicy Spring Greens Salad (recipe on page 43).

SERVES: 8 | **PREPARATION:** 15 minutes | **COOKING:** 30 minutes

1 cup (8 fl oz/250 ml) boiling water

4 sun-dried tomatoes (not oil-packed)

2½ lb (1.25 kg) red-skinned potatoes, cut into cubes

3 cups (24 fl oz/750 ml) water

2 cups (16 fl oz/500 ml) canned vegetable broth

½ teaspoon ground pepper

3 zucchini (courgettes), coarsely grated

⅓ cup (3 fl oz/80 ml) nonfat evaporated milk

⅓ cup (⅓ oz/10 g) chopped fresh basil or 1 teaspoon dried basil

◆ In a small bowl, pour the boiling water over the tomatoes. Let stand until the tomatoes are soft, about 5 minutes. Drain, then chop the tomatoes finely.

◆ In a large saucepan over high heat, bring the potatoes, water, broth, and pepper to a boil.

◆ Reduce heat to low, cover, and simmer, stirring occasionally, until the potatoes are tender, about 20 minutes.

◆ Remove from heat. Using a slotted spoon, transfer about half the potatoes to a medium bowl. Using a potato masher, mash until almost smooth. Return the mashed potatoes to the saucepan. Add the zucchini and stir to blend.

◆ Return the saucepan to medium heat, cover, and simmer, stirring once or twice, until the zucchini are tender and wilted, 5–7 minutes. Stir in the evaporated milk, basil, and chopped tomatoes.

◆ To serve, ladle into individual bowls.

Gingered carrot soup

Because carrots are available year-round, this soup is designed to suit every season. In cold weather, serve it steaming hot as a starter whose ginger aroma will entice diners. In warm weather, serve it chilled as a refreshing beverage with Quick Brown Bread (recipe on page 236).

SERVES: 6 | **PREPARATION:** 15 minutes + 4 hours if chilling | **COOKING:** 25 minutes

1 tablespoon olive oil

6 large carrots, peeled and cut into chunks

1 onion, thinly sliced

2 celery stalks, thinly sliced

3 tablespoons chopped celery leaves

2 cups (16 fl oz/500 ml) water

2 cups (16 fl oz/500 ml) canned vegetable broth

1 slice whole wheat (wholemeal) sandwich bread, torn into bits

1/4 cup (2 fl oz/60 ml) nonfat evaporated milk

1/2 cup (1/2 oz/15 g) thinly sliced green (spring) onion tops

2 tablespoons grated fresh ginger

◆ In a large saucepan over medium heat, heat the oil. Add the carrots, onion, celery, and celery leaves. Sauté for 5 minutes.

◆ Stir in the water, broth, and bread. Increase heat to high and bring to a boil.

◆ Reduce heat to low, cover, and simmer until the carrots are tender, about 20 minutes.

◆ Transfer the soup—in batches, if necessary—to a blender or food processor and purée until smooth.

◆ To serve hot, return the soup to the saucepan and stir in the milk and green onions. Reheat for a moment over low heat, not letting the soup boil, then stir in the ginger. Ladle into individual bowls.

◆ To serve cold, pour into a large bowl and stir in the milk, green onions, and ginger. Cool to room temperature, then cover and refrigerate until chilled thoroughly, at least 4 hours or up to 3 days. Ladle into mugs.

nutrition note

Carrots

Raw or cooked, carrots are an excellent source of beta-carotene, which your body changes to vitamin A. In fact, just one carrot provides about four times the recommended amount of vitamin A. Carrots are also a good source of dietary fiber.

Carrots will keep well for up to 2 weeks if they are refrigerated, unwashed, in a plastic bag; if you bought them with their green tops still attached, trim them off before storage, or the greens will deplete moisture from the roots.

Before cooking, scrub the carrots or peel them thinly using a vegetable peeler.

PER SERVING

Calories	105
Kilojoules	439
Protein	3 g
Carbohydrates	18 g
Total Fat	3 g
Saturated Fat	<1 g
Cholesterol	<1 mg
Sodium	419 mg
Dietary Fiber	4 g

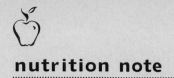
Split pea soup

Start a meal in style with Split Pea Soup paired with Tomato and Walnut Flat Bread (recipe on page 231). Adjust the addition of ground cloves to your taste, as the sweet, almost peppery spice is potent. For information on buying and storing spices and dried herbs, see page 168.

SERVES: 6 | **PREPARATION:** 15 minutes | **COOKING:** 70 minutes

2 cups (14 oz/440 g) green or yellow dried split peas

1 tablespoon olive oil

2 celery stalks, chopped

2 carrots, chopped

2 garlic cloves, minced

1 onion, chopped

1/2 teaspoon ground pepper

4 cups (32 fl oz/1 l) water, plus more if needed

2 cups (16 fl oz/500 ml) canned vegetable broth

1 bay leaf

1/2 teaspoon dried thyme

1/8 teaspoon ground cloves

♦ Place the split peas in a strainer and rinse under cold running water. Drain thoroughly.

♦ In a large saucepan over medium heat, heat the oil. Add the celery, carrots, garlic, onion, and pepper. Sauté until the vegetables are wilted, 5–7 minutes.

♦ Stir in the split peas, water, broth, bay leaf, thyme, and cloves. Increase heat to high and bring to a boil.

♦ Reduce heat to low, cover partially, and simmer, stirring occasionally, until the soup is thick and the peas are mushy, about 1 hour. If the soup seems too thick, stir in 1/4 cup (2 fl oz/60 ml) additional water. Remove and discard the bay leaf.

♦ To serve, ladle into individual bowls.

*a*ccording to the dictionary, a complement is any item that completes something else,
fills it up, or makes it perfect. The recipes in this
chapter for vegetables, grains, potatoes, and pastas fulfill
that definition deliciously. When it comes to "completing
something else," these dishes can play many roles. Use
them in the familiar role of side dish alongside a favorite
entree. Alternatively, serve two or more as a complete meal.
Or, have them as a single course in a multicourse meal.
Because grains, legumes, and vegetables are key compo-
nents of eating well, serving sizes for these complements
truly "fill you up." In most cases, the recipes in this chapter serve a generous 1 cup (8 ounces/250 grams), providing two of your recommended servings for the day. Adjust
the serving sizes to add or limit calories. Once you have
enjoyed these recipes in a meal, you'll agree that they
achieve the "makes it perfect" definition best of all.

complements

Stir-frying is a traditional Asian cooking technique that uses little or no oil. For successful stir-frying, follow these guidelines:

• *Cut ingredients into relatively small pieces of uniform size so they will cook quickly and evenly.*

• *Have all ingredients prepared and close to the stove to add easily during the fast cooking process.*

• *Cook over high heat using a nonstick wok, the traditional hemispherical Chinese pan, or a large frying pan.*

• *If using oil, add only enough to form a thin film in the pan. Or, use wine, broth, or nonstick cooking spray, as in this recipe.*

• *Add ingredients, starting with those that require the longest cooking time and ending with those that require the least.*

• *Stir in liquids and seasonings toward the end of cooking.*

Sesame asparagus-and-carrot stir-fry

The best Asian sesame oil is powerfully reminiscent of toasted sesame seeds and neither harsh nor bitter. Buy it in small bottles and keep trying new ones until you find the brand you like best. Remember, it takes just a small amount of sesame oil to impart its nutty flavor.

SERVES: 6 | **PREPARATION:** 15 minutes | **COOKING:** 10 minutes

24 asparagus

6 large carrots

1/4 cup (2 fl oz/60 ml) water

1 tablespoon grated fresh ginger

1 tablespoon reduced-sodium soy sauce

1 1/2 teaspoons sesame oil

1 tablespoon sesame seeds, toasted (see page 127)

◆ Cut the asparagus into 1/2-inch-thick (12-mm) slices. Cut the carrots into 1/4-inch-thick (6-mm) slices.

◆ Coat a nonstick wok or a large frying pan with nonstick cooking spray and place over high heat. Add the carrots and stir-fry for 4 minutes. Add the asparagus and water and stir and toss to combine. Cover and cook until the vegetables are barely tender, about 2 minutes.

◆ Uncover and add the ginger. Stir-fry until any remaining water evaporates, 1–2 minutes.

◆ Add the soy sauce, sesame oil, and sesame seeds. Stir-fry to coat the vegetables evenly.

◆ To serve, divide among individual plates.

PER SERVING

Calories	65
Kilojoules	272
Protein	3 g
Carbohydrates	10 g
Total Fat	2 g
Saturated Fat	<1 g
Cholesterol	0 mg
Sodium	127 mg
Dietary Fiber	3 g

Corn and lima bean medley

Because it uses nonfat evaporated milk rather than cream, this quick version of New England succotash has less fat than traditional recipes. It is one of the rare vegetable dishes that you can make ahead and reheat, using a double boiler, without loss of taste or texture.

SERVES: 6 | **PREPARATION:** 10 minutes | **COOKING:** 15 minutes

1 teaspoon cornstarch
(cornflour)

1 teaspoon sugar

1/4 teaspoon ground pepper

1 cup (8 fl oz/250 ml) nonfat
evaporated milk

2 cups (12 oz/375 g) fresh
corn kernels or frozen corn
kernels, thawed

10 oz (315 g) frozen lima
beans, thawed

1/4 cup (1 1/2 oz/45 g)
minced shallots

2 tablespoons chopped fresh
flat-leaf (Italian) parsley

◆ In a heavy saucepan, whisk together the cornstarch, sugar, and pepper until blended and smooth. Gradually whisk in the evaporated milk. Add the corn, lima beans, and shallots and stir to combine.

◆ Place over high heat and bring to a boil, stirring frequently. Reduce heat to low and simmer, stirring occasionally, until the vegetables are tender and the sauce has reduced by about half and coats the vegetables lightly, 10–12 minutes. Serve now, or refrigerate in a tightly covered container for up to 2 days.

◆ If needed, reheat in a double boiler.

◆ To serve, stir in the parsley and transfer to a bowl.

cooking clinic

Using a double boiler

Dairy products can scorch when heated in a pan placed directly on a stove's burner. To prevent scorching, use a double boiler. Double boilers are sold in kitchenware stores or houseware departments, but you can also improvise one using a saucepan and a heatproof bowl that fits over it.

• To use a double boiler, bring about 3 inches (7.5 cm) of water to a boil in the bottom of the double boiler or pan, then reduce heat to a simmer.

• Put the food to be reheated in the upper pan or a bowl and place on top, making sure its bottom is not in direct contact with the water.

• Stir frequently as the heat of the steam gently cooks or heats the food.

PER SERVING

Calories	142
Kilojoules	595
Protein	8 g
Carbohydrates	27 g
Total Fat	<1 g
Saturated Fat	<1 g
Cholesterol	2 mg
Sodium	86 mg
Dietary Fiber	5 g

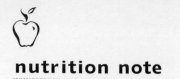

Beets à l'orange

Shredded beets cook in a fraction of the time of whole beets. To shred beets, first peel them, then use the large holes of a grater or a food processor fitted with the shredding blade. Pair the beets with Barley, Bell Pepper, and Almond Pilaf (recipe on page 100) for a meatless meal of complements.

SERVES: 4 | **PREPARATION:** 10 minutes | **COOKING:** 15 minutes

½ cup (4 fl oz/125 ml) water

2 teaspoons sugar

¼ teaspoon ground pepper

1½ lb (750 g) beets, peeled and shredded

3 tablespoons cider vinegar

1 tablespoon grated orange zest

♦ In a large frying pan over medium-high heat, bring the water, sugar, and pepper to a boil. Stir in the beets. Cover and cook for 5 minutes, stirring once.

♦ Uncover and continue cooking, stirring occasionally, until the water has mostly evaporated and the beets are tender, 5–7 minutes longer. Stir in the vinegar and orange zest.

♦ To serve, transfer to a serving bowl.

PER SERVING

Calories	64
Kilojoules	268
Protein	2 g
Carbohydrates	15 g
Total Fat	<1 g
Saturated Fat	<1 g
Cholesterol	0 mg
Sodium	86 mg
Dietary Fiber	1 g

Braised bok choy and cucumber

Brief cooking brings out the subtle flavor of cucumber, which combines with bok choy to make a refreshing dish served here with a broiled salmon fillet. If you can't find baby bok choy, substitute 3 cups (6 oz/185 g) chopped Swiss chard, beet greens, or spinach.

SERVES: 6 | **PREPARATION:** 15 minutes | **COOKING:** 10 minutes

2 cucumbers, each about 6 inches (15 cm) long, peeled

2 heads baby bok choy, each about 6 inches (15 cm) long

1 teaspoon olive oil

1/4 teaspoon ground pepper

1/4 cup (2 fl oz/60 ml) water

3 tablespoons chopped fresh dill or 1 teaspoon dried dill

♦ Halve the cucumbers lengthwise and scoop out the seeds. Cut the cucumbers crosswise into 1/2-inch-thick (12-mm) pieces. Slice the heads of the bok choy—leaves, stems, and all—crosswise into 1/2-inch-thick (12-mm) pieces.

♦ Coat a large frying pan with nonstick cooking spray and place over medium-high heat. Add the olive oil and, when hot, add the cucumbers and pepper. Sauté until the cucumbers have softened slightly yet retain some crunch, 5–7 minutes.

♦ Add the water and bok choy and increase heat to high. Continue cooking, stirring and tossing a few times, until the bok choy is wilted and tender and most of the liquid has evaporated, 2–3 minutes. Stir in the dill.

♦ To serve, divide among individual plates.

PER SERVING

Calories	22
Kilojoules	92
Protein	1 g
Carbohydrates	3 g
Total Fat	<1 g
Saturated Fat	<1 g
Cholesterol	0 mg
Sodium	23 mg
Dietary Fiber	<1 g

Caraway cabbage and cranberries

Dried cranberries are made from the tart fruit that is also used to make juice and sauce. Like other dried fruit, these jewels are relatively high in calories. The small amount here adds a subtle sweetness to a warm slaw. This dish is wonderful paired with pork or poultry dishes.

SERVES: 6 | **PREPARATION:** 15 minutes | **COOKING:** 20 minutes

1½ lb (750 g) green or red cabbage, quartered and cored

2 teaspoons olive oil

1 onion, thinly sliced

1 carrot, shredded

2 apples, preferably Golden Delicious, cored and shredded

¼ cup (1 oz/30 g) dried cranberries, chopped

½ teaspoon ground pepper

½ teaspoon caraway seeds

⅓ cup (3 fl oz/80 ml) malt vinegar or cider vinegar

2 tablespoons sugar

½ cup (4 fl oz/125 ml) water

2 tablespoons chopped fresh flat-leaf (Italian) parsley

♦ Using a sharp knife or a food processor fitted with the slicing disk, shred the cabbage.

♦ In a large saucepan over medium heat, heat the olive oil. Add the onion and carrot and sauté until softened slightly, about 5 minutes.

♦ Add the cabbage, apples, cranberries, pepper, caraway seeds, vinegar, sugar, and water. Stir and toss to combine. Bring to a boil. Reduce heat to medium, cover, and cook, stirring occasionally, until the cabbage is tender and the liquid has mostly evaporated, about 15 minutes. Stir in the parsley.

♦ Serve now, or refrigerate in a tightly covered container for up to 24 hours. Although delicious freshly cooked, this combination seems to taste even better after the various elements have had a chance to mingle.

♦ If needed, reheat in a double boiler (see page 71).

♦ To serve, transfer to a bowl.

PER SERVING

Calories	112
Kilojoules	467
Protein	2 g
Carbohydrates	24 g
Total Fat	2 g
Saturated Fat	<1 g
Cholesterol	0 mg
Sodium	22 mg
Dietary Fiber	4 g

Baked breaded tomatoes

Tomatoes are the most popular vegetable worldwide. Any type of fresh tomato will work in this recipe, but Romas are particularly nice because they are firmer, less juicy, and have a consistently better flavor than many other varieties.

SERVES: 6 | **PREPARATION:** 15 minutes | **COOKING:** 30 minutes | **COOLING:** 5 minutes

5 slices whole wheat (whole-meal) sandwich bread, made into crumbs

2 tablespoons grated Parmesan cheese

1 tablespoon olive oil

2 tablespoons chopped fresh flat-leaf (Italian) parsley

1 tablespoon chopped fresh oregano or 1½ teaspoons dried oregano

12 Roma (plum) tomatoes, quartered lengthwise

4 green (spring) onions, thinly sliced, including green portions

½ teaspoon ground pepper

1 teaspoon sugar

◆ Preheat an oven to 375°F (190°C). Coat a glass or ceramic 8-inch (20-cm) baking dish with nonstick cooking spray.

◆ In a bowl, combine the crumbs, cheese, olive oil, parsley, and oregano. Stir and toss vigorously to coat the crumbs evenly.

◆ In a large nonstick frying pan over medium-high heat, combine the tomatoes, onions, pepper, and sugar. Sauté until the tomatoes soften slightly and exude some juice, 8–10 minutes.

◆ Spread half the tomato mixture over the bottom of the prepared baking dish, then sprinkle with half the crumb mixture. Spoon the remaining tomato mixture over the crumbs, then sprinkle the remaining crumbs evenly over the top.

◆ Bake until the crumb topping is crisp and browned, about 20 minutes.

◆ Cool 5 minutes before serving.

Making bread crumbs

Bread crumbs are an excellent way to add grains to your meal.

Choose a loaf of whole wheat (wholemeal) bread with a firm, coarse-textured crumb. If you want a finer consistency to the crumbs, trim away the crusts; this step is not necessary, however, for more rustic or home-style dishes. With your hands, crumble the bread into a blender or food processor. Pulse the machine on and off until the crumbs reach the desired consistency.

If you like drier crumbs for a crunchier consistency, spread them in a baking dish or on a baking sheet and put them in an oven set at its lowest temperature. Bake for about 1 hour, stirring occasionally, or until they feel thoroughly dry to the touch.

PER SERVING

Calories	120
Kilojoules	501
Protein	4 g
Carbohydrates	18 g
Total Fat	4 g
Saturated Fat	<1 g
Cholesterol	1 mg
Sodium	169 mg
Dietary Fiber	4 g

Preparing chestnuts

Shelling and peeling fresh chestnuts is a chore that some cooks find satisfying while others find strenuous. If you are among the latter, and don't mind the cost, look for roasted and peeled whole chestnuts or chestnut pieces in specialty-food shops.

To roast and peel chestnuts yourself, follow these steps:

• *Preheat an oven to 400°F (200°C).*

• *With a sharp knife, carefully score an X in the shell on the flat side of each chestnut.*

• *Spread the chestnuts in a baking pan in a single layer. Bake until the shells begin to turn brittle and peel back slightly at the X, about 15 minutes.*

• *Cool slightly, just to the touch; they must be peeled while still warm. Wearing kitchen gloves, if necessary, peel off the shells and the furry skins beneath them.*

Brussels sprouts and chestnuts

In winter, Brussels sprouts are among your best vegetable choices. Here, the tiny cabbages are topped with a combination of milk and cornstarch, which forms a sauce with a creamlike consistency. Serve this elegant complement in a starring role at special-occasion meals.

SERVES: 6 | **PREPARATION:** 10 minutes | **COOKING:** 30 minutes

1½ lb (750 g) Brussels sprouts

⅓ cup (3 fl oz/80 ml) canned vegetable broth

⅓ cup (3 fl oz/80 ml) water

¾ teaspoon chopped fresh thyme or ¼ teaspoon dried thyme

¼ teaspoon ground pepper

1½ cups (8 oz/250 g) peeled, shelled, cooked chestnuts

2 teaspoons cornstarch (cornflour)

⅔ cup (5 fl oz/160 ml) nonfat evaporated milk

1 tablespoon chopped fresh flat-leaf (Italian) parsley

◆ Remove any blemished outer leaves from the Brussels sprouts. Depending on their size, halve or quarter them lengthwise to make fairly uniform pieces.

◆ In a large saucepan over high heat, bring the sprouts, broth, water, thyme, and pepper to a boil. Reduce heat to medium-low, cover, and cook until the sprouts are tender, about 20 minutes.

◆ Add the chestnuts and cook, uncovered, stirring occasionally, until the liquid has mostly evaporated, about 3 minutes.

◆ In a small bowl, whisk together the cornstarch and milk until smooth. Add to the simmering vegetables. Increase the heat to high and cook, stirring frequently, until thickened, about 3 minutes.

◆ To serve, transfer to a bowl. Sprinkle with the parsley.

PER SERVING

Calories	126
Kilojoules	525
Protein	7 g
Carbohydrates	25 g
Total Fat	<1 g
Saturated Fat	<1 g
Cholesterol	1 mg
Sodium	127 mg
Dietary Fiber	7 g

Tender spring peas and asparagus

Quick cooking in broth captures the sweet taste of these calling cards of fair weather: peas and asparagus. With a dash of red bell pepper for contrasting color, this lovely dish can star on any spring table. Because fresh peas have the briefest of seasons, use frozen peas when necessary.

SERVES: 6 | **PREPARATION:** 10 minutes | **COOKING:** 10 minutes

32 asparagus

²/₃ cup (5 fl oz/160 ml) water

¹/₃ cup (3 fl oz/80 ml) canned vegetable broth

3 shallots, minced

2 lb (1 kg) fresh peas, shelled or 10 oz (315 g) frozen peas

¹/₄ teaspoon ground pepper

¹/₂ red bell pepper (capsicum), seeded, stemmed, and diced

♦ Cut the asparagus into 1-inch-thick (2.5-cm) pieces.

♦ In a large frying pan over medium-high heat, bring the water, broth, and shallots to a boil. Stir in the asparagus, peas, and ground pepper. Cover and cook for 5 minutes.

♦ Uncover, add the bell pepper, and cook until the liquid has mostly evaporated, about 2 minutes.

♦ To serve, transfer to a bowl.

nutrition note

Asparagus

A special treat of springtime and early summer, tender-crisp spears of asparagus are, in fact, the immature shoots of a tuber that is a member of the lily family.

Distinctively rich in flavor, asparagus also contains vitamin C plus folic acid (folate).

To preserve its nutrients, wrap asparagus in a damp paper towel and place in a plastic bag in the refrigerator. You'll preserve all of the folic acid (folate) and most of the vitamin C for up to 5 days.

PER SERVING

Calories	79
Kilojoules	332
Protein	7 g
Carbohydrates	14 g
Total Fat	<1 g
Saturated Fat	<1 g
Cholesterol	0 mg
Sodium	61 mg
Dietary Fiber	4 g

Choosing kasha

The term kasha refers to the dried triangular seeds of the buckwheat flower, which is not at all related to wheat and isn't even a true grain. Kasha is sold whole or, more commonly, ground into particles called "groats" in coarse, medium, or fine granulation. Medium granulation kasha is used for the recipes in this book. All kasha is noted for its nutty flavor, which has a slight, pleasantly sour edge.

You can find kasha near the rice and other grains in well-stocked markets and natural foods shops, as well as in Jewish delicatessens and Eastern European food stores. It is also the source of the flour used to make Japanese soba noodles (see page 128).

Store kasha in a tightly covered container away from heat and light, preferably in the refrigerator or freezer, for up to 2 months.

Corn and kasha cakes

Offer these fiber-filled pancakes, 2 to a serving, as a side dish, light lunch, or appetizer. Eat them plain or use them as a base for a multitude of toppings, including lowfat cream cheese or cottage cheese or Fresh Tomato Salsa (recipe on page 99), as shown here.

MAKES: 12 | **PREPARATION:** 15 minutes | **SOAKING:** 10 minutes | **COOKING:** 20 minutes

1/4 cup (2 oz/60 g) kasha, medium granulation

1/2 cup (4 fl oz/125 ml) boiling water

1 1/4 cups (7 oz/220 g) fresh corn kernels or frozen corn kernels, thawed

1 egg

3/4 cup (6 fl oz/180 ml) lowfat buttermilk

1/8 teaspoon cayenne pepper

1/3 cup (2 oz/60 g) all-purpose (plain) flour

1/3 cup (2 oz/60 g) whole wheat (wholemeal) flour

1/2 teaspoon baking powder

1/4 teaspoon baking soda (bicarbonate of soda)

◆ In a small bowl, stir together the kasha and boiling water and let stand for 10 minutes.

◆ In a blender or food processor, combine half of the corn kernels, the egg, buttermilk, cayenne, flour, baking powder, and baking soda. Process until the batter is smooth, about 30 seconds. Add the remaining corn and the kasha. Stir briefly to combine.

◆ Coat a large nonstick frying pan with nonstick cooking spray and place over medium heat. When a drop of water sizzles as it hits the pan, spoon in a scant 1/4 cup (2 fl oz/60 ml) batter for each cake. Cook until the cakes are dry around the edges and a few small bubbles form on top, about 2 minutes. Turn and cook until browned on the other side, about 1 1/2 minutes longer.

◆ Transfer to a platter. Cover loosely with aluminum foil and keep warm while cooking the remaining cakes.

PER CAKE

Calories	67
Kilojoules	279
Protein	3 g
Carbohydrates	12 g
Total Fat	1 g
Saturated Fat	<1 g
Cholesterol	19 mg
Sodium	76 mg
Dietary Fiber	1 g

Celery root and apple purée

While its color and texture resemble applesauce, this wintry purée is a savory vegetable complement. Try it paired with pork, as shown here, or with roasted or steamed vegetables. The watercress sprig garnish is an example of enhancing a dish with a flavorful herb rather than a dash of salt.

SERVES: 6 | **PREPARATION:** 15 minutes | **COOKING:** 30 minutes

2 lb (1 kg) celery root (celeriac), peeled and cut into chunks

2 large apples such as Golden Delicious or Gala, cored and cut into chunks

1 onion, coarsely chopped

1/2 cup (4 fl oz/125 ml) lowfat buttermilk

1/4 cup (2 fl oz/60 ml) thawed unsweetened apple juice concentrate

1/4 teaspoon ground nutmeg

1/4 teaspoon ground white pepper

6 watercress sprigs

◆ In a large pot fitted with a steamer basket, bring 2 inches (5 cm) water to a boil. Add the celery root, apples, and onion. Reduce heat to medium, cover, and steam until the fruit and vegetables are very tender, 25–30 minutes.

◆ In a food processor or blender, process the celery root, apples, and onion—working in batches, if necessary—until a coarse purée is formed. Transfer to a warmed bowl. Stir in the buttermilk, apple juice concentrate, nutmeg, and pepper.

◆ If needed, reheat in a double boiler (see page 71).

◆ To serve, divide among individual plates. Garnish with a watercress sprig.

nutrition note

Celery root

Widely used in southern Europe a century ago or longer, celery root (celeriac) is making a culinary comeback today.

Its popularity is thanks to its combination of refreshing flavor reminiscent of the crisp celery stalks that grow from a related plant, rich texture that lends itself well to puréeing, low calorie count, and almost total lack of fat.

PER SERVING

Calories	119
Kilojoules	496
Protein	3 g
Carbohydrates	28 g
Total Fat	<1 g
Saturated Fat	<1 g
Cholesterol	1 mg
Sodium	163 mg
Dietary Fiber	1 g

Spinach

Mention spinach and most people think of Popeye, the cartoon character who downs a canful whenever he needs a burst of strength. Such powers are attributed to the vegetable's abundant iron, a mineral essential to building hemoglobin, which carries oxygen through your blood.

Spinach is, indeed, iron-rich, but it also contains oxalic acid. Because oxalic acid binds iron, only a small amount of the iron in spinach may actually be absorbed by your body. Spinach does, however, contain beta-carotene. A 1/2-cup (3 1/2-oz/105-g) cooked serving has more than a day's supply of this important antioxidant. It also contains vitamin C, folic acid (folate), and dietary fiber.

Lemon zest spinach

Many Japanese restaurants offer a version of this zesty dish as an appetizer. It makes a great complement to other vegetables, meat, or seafood. Prepare it in minutes using packaged washed spinach. For this recipe, be sure the leaves are completely dry before cooking.

SERVES: 6 | **PREPARATION:** 10 minutes | **COOKING:** 10 minutes

1 teaspoon olive oil

2 green (spring) onions, chopped, including green portions

2 garlic cloves, minced

1 1/4 lb (625 g) fresh spinach leaves, clean, dry, and stemmed

1 1/2 tablespoons balsamic vinegar

3 teaspoons grated lemon zest

1 teaspoon sesame seeds, toasted (see page 127)

♦ In a large stockpot over medium heat, heat the olive oil. Add the green onions and garlic and cook, stirring, until softened slightly, about 1 minute.

♦ Add the spinach leaves, packing them in. If you can't fit them all at once, cover the pan for about 30 seconds to wilt the spinach a little, then add the remaining spinach in batches. Cover the pan tightly and cook, stirring once or twice, until all the spinach is wilted and tender but still bright green, 3–5 minutes.

♦ Remove from heat. Add the vinegar and lemon zest and stir to combine.

♦ To serve, transfer to a platter. Sprinkle with the sesame seeds. Serve hot or cold.

PER SERVING

Calories	29
Kilojoules	123
Protein	2 g
Carbohydrates	4 g
Total Fat	1 g
Saturated Fat	<1 g
Cholesterol	0 mg
Sodium	55 mg
Dietary Fiber	2 g

Deviled cauliflower

The word "deviled" indicates that a dish includes mustard and spices. This flavorful, lowfat mustard-based topping adds a devilish twist to steamed and then baked cauliflower. Serve it as a complement to pasta or grain dishes. Try the same topping and technique with other cruciferous vegetables.

SERVES: 6 | **PREPARATION:** 15 minutes | **COOKING:** 30 minutes

⅓ cup (3 oz/90 g) plain nonfat yogurt

¼ cup (1 oz/30 g) grated Parmesan cheese

¼ cup (2 fl oz/60 ml) Dijon mustard

¼ teaspoon dried tarragon

1 slice whole wheat (wholemeal) sandwich bread, made into crumbs (see page 79)

1 tablespoon chopped fresh tarragon or 1 teaspoon dried tarragon

1 teaspoon olive oil

2 lb (1 kg) cauliflower, cut into florets

♦ Preheat an oven to 375°F (190°C). Coat an 8-inch (20-cm) square baking pan with nonstick cooking spray.

♦ In a small bowl, stir together the yogurt, cheese, mustard, and dried tarragon.

♦ In another bowl, combine the bread crumbs, tarragon, and olive oil. Stir vigorously to coat the crumbs with oil.

♦ In a large pot fitted with a steamer basket, bring 2 inches (5 cm) water to a boil. Add the cauliflower, reduce heat to medium, cover, and steam until just tender, about 8 minutes. Spread the cauliflower evenly in the prepared pan.

♦ Spoon the mustard mixture over the cauliflower and stir gently to coat. Sprinkle the bread crumbs over the top. Bake until the crumbs are crisp and well browned, 15–20 minutes.

♦ To serve, divide among individual plates.

PER SERVING

Calories	74
Kilojoules	310
Protein	4 g
Carbohydrates	6 g
Total Fat	3 g
Saturated Fat	1 g
Cholesterol	4 mg
Sodium	373 mg
Dietary Fiber	2 g

Simmering green beans

Cooking green beans in a large amount of water dilutes the acids in the vegetable to prevent or at least reduce the formation of a chemical that makes green beans turn brown.

In this recipe, the nutrients that cook out of the vegetables are preserved in the cooking liquid and served as part of the "stew."

To be sure to capture all its flavorful liquid, serve this simmered stew in a small bowl or over a grain in a soup plate.

Green bean and tomato stew

Green beans, also known as string beans or snap beans, are one of spring's and summer's most widely available vegetables. While fresh vegetables will give you the best results, this is one recipe in which frozen beans and canned tomatoes also work well.

SERVES: 6 | **PREPARATION:** 20 minutes | **COOKING:** 20 minutes

1¼ lb (625 g) green beans, trimmed

1¼ cups (10 fl oz/310 ml) water

¼ teaspoon ground pepper

2 large tomatoes, coarsely chopped

1½ teaspoons chopped fresh thyme or ½ teaspoon dried thyme

6 green (spring) onions, thinly sliced, including green portions

♦ Cut the green beans into 2-inch-long (5-cm) pieces.

♦ In a large saucepan over high heat, bring the beans, water, and pepper to a boil. Reduce heat to low, cover, and simmer for 10 minutes.

♦ Add the tomatoes, thyme, and half the green onions. Cover and simmer until the tomatoes and beans are very tender, 5–7 minutes.

♦ To serve, divide among individual bowls. Top each with an equal amount of the remaining green onions.

PER SERVING

Calories	45
Kilojoules	189
Protein	2 g
Carbohydrates	10 g
Total Fat	<1 g
Saturated Fat	<1 g
Cholesterol	0 mg
Sodium	13 mg
Dietary Fiber	3 g

Fragrant fennel in fresh fig sauce

The fresh figs disintegrate during cooking, forming a pretty purple sauce to spoon over the gently braised fennel. Here, the elegant complement is served on its own. Use any type of fresh fig you can find. When fresh figs are not available, substitute 3 cups (20 oz/625 g) canned figs.

SERVES: 6 | **PREPARATION:** 10 minutes | **COOKING:** 30 minutes

6 small fennel bulbs, 3 lb (1.5 kg) total, trimmed

1/2 cup (4 fl oz/125 ml) canned vegetable broth

1 cup (8 fl oz/250 ml) water

1/8 teaspoon salt

6 fresh figs, stemmed and coarsely chopped

1 1/2 tablespoons balsamic vinegar

1/4 teaspoon ground pepper

1 tablespoon chopped fresh flat-leaf (Italian) parsley

◆ Cut each fennel bulb in half lengthwise through the base, then cut each piece in half again. Remove the outer pieces of the bulbs if they look tough or stringy.

◆ Coat a large nonstick frying pan with nonstick cooking spray. Place over medium-high heat. Add the fennel in a single layer and cook, turning, until lightly browned on all sides, 2–3 minutes.

◆ Add the broth, water, salt, and figs. Reduce heat to low, cover, and simmer until the fennel is tender, about 20 minutes.

◆ Stir in the vinegar and pepper. Increase heat to medium-high and cook, stirring occasionally, until the sauce has thickened slightly, 5–7 minutes.

◆ To serve, divide the fennel among individual plates. Top each with an equal amount of the fig sauce. Sprinkle with the parsley.

cooking clinic

Enjoying fennel

Resembling a rounded, swollen cluster of celery stalks with green-tinged ribs, this vegetable, available in most stores year-round, is related to the herb and spice seeds of the same name. All share a mild, sweet licorice flavor. People have enjoyed both raw and cooked fennel in Mediterranean lands since the days of ancient Greece and Rome.

Strip away any coarse outer portions of fennel bulbs before using them in recipes.

Fennel bulb is also sometimes known as finocchio, its Italian name, or sweet anise.

PER SERVING

Calories	90
Kilojoules	377
Protein	3 g
Carbohydrates	20 g
Total Fat	<1 g
Saturated Fat	0 g
Cholesterol	0 mg
Sodium	315 mg
Dietary Fiber	4 g

Broccoli in spicy orange sauce

Many recipes call for broccoli florets, ignoring the stems. When properly trimmed and peeled, however, broccoli stems are perfectly edible and supply all the same nutrients as the florets. Some people even prefer the slightly sweeter taste and crunchier texture of the stems.

SERVES: 6 | **PREPARATION:** 15 minutes | **COOKING:** 10 minutes

2 lb (1 kg) broccoli

½ cup (4 fl oz/125 ml) orange juice

2 teaspoons honey

1 teaspoon Dijon mustard

1 teaspoon grated orange zest

½ teaspoon reduced-sodium soy sauce

1 garlic clove, crushed with a garlic press

⅛ teaspoon red pepper flakes

1½ teaspoons cornstarch

1 tablespoon water

1 teaspoon sesame seeds, toasted (see page 127)

♦ Trim the broccoli florets into pieces about 1½ inches (4 cm) long. Cut the stalks crosswise into pieces about ⅓ inch (9 mm) thick.

♦ In a large pot fitted with a steamer basket, bring 2 inches (5 cm) water to a boil. Add the stalks, cover, and steam for 2 minutes. Add the florets and steam for 5 minutes longer.

♦ Meanwhile, in a small saucepan over medium high heat, bring the orange juice, honey, mustard, orange zest, soy sauce, garlic, and pepper flakes to a boil.

♦ In a small bowl, whisk together the cornstarch and water. Stir into the orange juice mixture and cook until thickened, about 1 minute.

♦ To serve, in a serving bowl, gently toss the broccoli with the sauce to coat. Sprinkle with the sesame seeds.

PER SERVING

Calories	67
Kilojoules	279
Protein	5 g
Carbohydrates	13 g
Total Fat	<1 g
Saturated Fat	<1 g
Cholesterol	0 mg
Sodium	78 mg
Dietary Fiber	4 g

Roasted peppers and basil

Roasted bell peppers have a tender, juicy texture and a sweet flavor. To use roasted peppers in other recipes, prepare them through step 3. You can also roast them ahead and refrigerate in a tightly covered container for up to 1 week. Rinse commercially prepared peppers to reduce salt before use.

SERVES: 6 | **PREPARATION:** 15 minutes | **COOKING:** 20 minutes | **MARINATING:** 30 minutes

3 red bell peppers (capsicums)

3 green bell peppers (capsicums)

3 yellow bell peppers (capsicums)

1/2 cup (1/2 oz/15 g) loosely packed fresh basil leaves

1 1/2 tablespoons balsamic vinegar

3 garlic cloves, crushed with a garlic press

♦ Preheat a broiler (griller).

♦ Place the whole peppers under the broiler. Broil, turning frequently, until all sides are blackened and blistered, 10–20 minutes. Transfer the peppers to a paper bag and seal to close. Cool for 15 minutes, then scrape the blackened skin from the peppers.

♦ Halve the peppers and remove the seeds, stems, and ribs. Cut lengthwise into 1/2-inch-wide (12-mm) strips.

♦ In a large bowl, combine the pepper strips, basil, vinegar, and garlic. Toss to mix well. Cover and marinate for 30 minutes at room temperature before serving.

PER SERVING

Calories	33
Kilojoules	139
Protein	1 g
Carbohydrates	8 g
Total Fat	<1 g
Saturated Fat	0 g
Cholesterol	0 mg
Sodium	3 mg
Dietary Fiber	2 g

Fresh tomato salsa

Using this simple recipe, you can make a quick salsa to fit your taste and the available ingredients, adding or subtracting chiles and onions as you desire. Unlike many purchased versions of salsa, this quick concoction is very low in sodium.

MAKES: 2 cups (12 oz/375 g) | **PREPARATION:** 10 minutes

2 tomatoes

1/2 red (Spanish) onion

2 green (spring) onions

1 garlic clove, minced

1/2 jalapeño chile, seeded and minced

3 tablespoons chopped cilantro (fresh coriander)

3 tablespoons red or white wine vinegar

♦ Chop the tomatoes and red onion into equal-sized pieces. Finely chop the green onion, including green portions.

♦ In a large bowl, stir together the tomatoes, onions, garlic, jalapeño, cilantro, and vinegar. Serve now, or refrigerate in a tightly covered container for up to 3 days.

PER TABLESPOON

Calories	27
Kilojoules	113
Protein	1 g
Carbohydrates	6 g
Total Fat	<1 g
Saturated Fat	0 g
Cholesterol	0 mg
Sodium	10 mg
Dietary Fiber	1 g

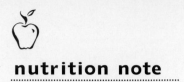
Barley, bell pepper, and almond pilaf

Barley, a grain originating in the Middle East, is commonly added to soups. In this recipe, however, pearl barley is used to make a pilaf. For a fluffy texture, avoid stirring the barley while it simmers, so that less of the surface starch dissolves in the cooking liquid.

SERVES: 6 | **PREPARATION:** 15 minutes | **COOKING:** 35 minutes

2 teaspoons olive oil

1 small onion, chopped

1 small green bell pepper (capsicum), seeded, stemmed, and chopped

1 cup (6 oz/185 g) pearl barley

1/4 teaspoon ground pepper

1 cup (8 fl oz/250 ml) canned vegetable broth

2 cups (16 fl oz/500 ml) water

2 tablespoons slivered almonds, toasted (see page 127)

♦ In a large frying pan over medium heat, heat the olive oil. Add the onion and bell pepper and sauté until wilted, about 4 minutes.

♦ Add the barley and pepper and sauté for 3 minutes.

♦ Stir in the broth and water and bring to a boil. Reduce heat to low, cover, and simmer until the barley is tender and the liquid is absorbed, about 25 minutes.

♦ To serve, transfer to a bowl and garnish with the slivered almonds.

PER SERVING

Calories	143
Kilojoules	598
Protein	4 g
Carbohydrates	25 g
Total Fat	3 g
Saturated Fat	<1 g
Cholesterol	0 mg
Sodium	170 mg
Dietary Fiber	5 g

Oyster mushroom and barley risotto

Traditionally, the Italian rice dish known as risotto includes a considerable amount of cheese. This version lets you enjoy the soft texture of grain and melted cheese with a fraction of the calories. Oyster mushrooms give the recipe a flavor reminiscent of seafood, but you can use any mushroom.

SERVES: 6 | **PREPARATION:** 10 minutes | **COOKING:** 1 hour

6 cups (48 fl oz/1.5 l) water

2/3 cup (4 oz/125 g) short-grain brown rice

2/3 cup (4 oz/125 g) pearl barley

1 teaspoon olive oil

1 lb (500 g) oyster mushrooms, thinly sliced

1/2 cup (4 fl oz/125 ml) canned vegetable broth

1/4 cup (1 oz/30 g) grated Parmesan cheese

1/4 teaspoon ground pepper

◆ In a large, heavy saucepan, bring the water to a boil. Add the rice and barley and return to a boil, stirring frequently. Reduce heat to low and simmer, uncovered, stirring occasionally, until the barley and rice are tender and have absorbed most of the water, about 50 minutes.

◆ About 10 minutes before the rice and barley are done, heat the olive oil in a large frying pan over medium heat. Add the mushrooms and sauté until barely tender, 8–10 minutes.

◆ Add the barley-rice mixture to the mushrooms and stir to combine. Add the broth, cheese, and pepper. Stir until the cheese melts and the mixture is creamy.

◆ To serve, divide among individual plates.

nutrition note

Barley

Pearl barley is so named because its heavy, unpalatable hulls and bran have been stripped away, leaving almost-spherical grains that are steamed and polished to a pearly sheen. Like the Arborio variety of rice traditionally used in risotto, pearl barley releases ample surface starch during cooking, resulting in a sauce whose creamy taste and texture belie how low in fat it is.

Despite the removal of its outer coating, barley is still an excellent source of dietary fiber, providing a generous 3 grams per 1/2-cup (3 3/4-oz/110-g) cooked serving.

PER SERVING

Calories	178
Kilojoules	747
Protein	7 g
Carbohydrates	33 g
Total Fat	3 g
Saturated Fat	1 g
Cholesterol	4 mg
Sodium	176 mg
Dietary Fiber	5 g

Kasha and cremini mushrooms

Low-calorie mushrooms are a natural flavor enhancer, as proved by this quick dish. Toasting enhances any grain, bringing out its nutty flavor. For a satisfying meal, pair the cremini mushrooms and nutty-flavored kasha with a simple baked chicken breast.

SERVES: 6 | **PREPARATION:** 10 minutes | **COOKING:** 20 minutes

1½ cups (12 oz/375 g) kasha, medium granulation

2 teaspoons olive oil

8 oz (250 g) cremini mushrooms, sliced

1 onion, chopped

1 cup (8 fl oz/250 ml) canned vegetable broth

2 cups (16 fl oz/500 ml) water

1 tablespoon chopped fresh thyme or 1 teaspoon dried thyme

¼ teaspoon ground pepper

½ red bell pepper (capsicum), diced

1 tablespoon chopped fresh flat-leaf (Italian) parsley

♦ In a heavy frying pan over medium-high heat, toast the kasha, stirring, until darkened slightly, 2–3 minutes. Remove from the heat.

♦ In a large nonstick frying pan over medium heat, heat the olive oil. Add the mushrooms and onion and sauté until softened, 3–5 minutes.

♦ In a small saucepan, bring the broth and water to a boil. Add to the mushroom mixture. Stir in the kasha, thyme, and pepper. Reduce heat to low, cover, and simmer until the kasha is just tender and all the liquid is absorbed, 8–10 minutes.

♦ To serve, stir in the bell pepper and parsley and transfer to a platter.

PER SERVING

Calories	257
Kilojoules	1,074
Protein	9 g
Carbohydrates	52 g
Total Fat	3 g
Saturated Fat	<1 g
Cholesterol	0 mg
Sodium	176 mg
Dietary Fiber	7 g

Squashes and brown rice primavera

Many of the recipes in this book, like this vegetable-filled dish, call for cooked rice. The technique at right uses a standard ratio of water to rice but eliminates the butter called for in many methods. To prevent the rice from clumping, cook it, cool it, then separate the grains before use.

SERVES: 6 | **PREPARATION:** 15 minutes | **COOKING:** 10 minutes

2 zucchini (courgettes)

2 yellow crookneck squashes

3 cups (15 oz/470 g) cooked, cold brown rice

2 garlic cloves, minced

1/2 teaspoon ground pepper

1/4 cup (2 fl oz/60 ml) water

1 large tomato, seeded and diced (see page 167)

1/2 cup (3/4 oz/20 g) chopped fresh basil

1/4 cup (1/2 oz/10 g) chopped fresh flat-leaf (Italian) parsley

1/4 cup (1 oz/30 g) grated Parmesan cheese

◆ Halve the zucchini and squashes lengthwise, then cut crosswise into 1/2-inch-thick (12-mm) pieces.

◆ Put the rice in a large bowl and gently separate the grains and break apart any lumps.

◆ Coat a large nonstick frying pan with nonstick cooking spray and place over medium-high heat. Add the garlic and sauté for 30 seconds. Add the zucchini, squash, and pepper and sauté for 3 minutes.

◆ Stir in the water, cover, and cook until the vegetables are tender when pierced, about 3 minutes.

◆ Uncover and add the rice. Cook, stirring constantly, until heated through, 3–4 minutes. Stir in the tomato, basil, parsley, and cheese.

◆ To serve, transfer to a platter.

PER SERVING

Calories	176
Kilojoules	736
Protein	6 g
Carbohydrates	32 g
Total Fat	3 g
Saturated Fat	1 g
Cholesterol	4 mg
Sodium	97 mg
Dietary Fiber	2 g

Binding with bread crumbs

The whole wheat (wholemeal) bread crumbs called for in this recipe perform an important culinary role. As an ingredient, the crumbs help bind the mixture together, just as rolled oats do in the recipe for Baked Vegetable-and-Turkey Loaf on page 192. Being smaller particles than the grains of brown rice, they also lighten the texture of the cakes.

Brown rice cakes

When cooking brown rice, make extra to use in these simple, soft cakes. Serve them hot or cold, topped with a dollop of Roasted Peppers and Basil (recipe on page 99) for a savory side dish. You can also eat them as a snack or as an alternative to bread in a sandwich.

MAKES: 12 | **PREPARATION:** 25 minutes | **COOKING:** 20 minutes

$1/3$ cup (2 oz/60 g) all-purpose (plain) flour

1 teaspoon baking powder

$1/2$ teaspoon ground pepper

3 slices whole wheat (wholemeal) sandwich bread, made into crumbs (see page 79)

1 cup (8 fl oz/250 ml) nonfat milk

1 egg

$1^{1}/3$ cups (7 oz/220 g) cooked, cold brown rice (see page 107)

$1/3$ cup ($1/3$ oz/10 g) chopped chives

♦ Preheat an oven to 350°F (180°C).

♦ Onto a piece of waxed paper, sift together the flour, baking powder, and pepper.

♦ Spread the bread crumbs in a shallow baking pan and toast them in the oven, stirring twice, until lightly browned, 12–15 minutes. Scrape the crumbs into a bowl. Stir in the milk and let stand for 5 minutes.

♦ Add the egg and rice and beat vigorously to separate the grains of rice and break apart any lumps. Stir in the chives. Stir in the combined dry ingredients. The batter will be quite stiff.

♦ Coat a large nonstick frying pan with nonstick cooking spray and place over medium heat. When a drop of water sizzles as it hits the pan, spoon in a scant $1/4$ cup (2 fl oz/60 ml) batter for each cake. Cook until the cakes are dry around the edges and a few small bubbles form on top, about 2 minutes. Turn and cook until browned on the other side, about $1^{1}/2$ minutes longer.

♦ Transfer to a platter, cover loosely with aluminum foil, and keep warm while cooking the remaining cakes.

PER RICE CAKE

Calories	69
Kilojoules	287
Protein	3 g
Carbohydrates	12 g
Total Fat	1 g
Saturated Fat	<1 g
Cholesterol	18 mg
Sodium	95 mg
Dietary Fiber	<1 g

Saffron rice and golden raisin pilaf

The lovely yellow spice saffron, the dried, hand-picked stigmas of a species of crocus, provides a rich golden color and distinctive flavor, but at a high price. Fortunately, a little goes a long way in flavoring this Middle Eastern recipe. For a more earthy flavored dish, substitute turmeric for the saffron.

SERVES: 6 | **PREPARATION:** 10 minutes | **COOKING:** 25 minutes

1 tablespoon olive oil

1 onion, chopped

1½ cups (10½ oz/330 g) long-grain white rice

1 cup (8 fl oz/250 ml) canned vegetable broth

2 cups (16 fl oz/500 ml) water

½ teaspoon ground pepper

¼ teaspoon ground cinnamon

¼ teaspoon ground allspice

½ cup (3 oz/90 g) golden raisins (sultanas)

¼ cup (1½ oz/45 g) dried currants

⅛ teaspoon saffron threads

2 tablespoons pine nuts, toasted (see page 127)

◆ In a large frying pan over medium heat, heat the olive oil. Add the onion and sauté until wilted, about 3 minutes. Add the rice and continue to sauté for 2 minutes.

◆ Add the broth, water, pepper, cinnamon, and allspice. Increase heat to high and bring to a boil.

◆ Stir in the raisins, currants, saffron, and half the pine nuts. Reduce heat to low, cover, and simmer until the rice is tender and has absorbed all the liquid, about 20 minutes.

◆ To serve, stir and fluff the rice, then transfer to a platter. Garnish with the remaining pine nuts.

PER SERVING

Calories	294
Kilojoules	1,231
Protein	5 g
Carbohydrates	60 g
Total Fat	4 g
Saturated Fat	<1 g
Cholesterol	0 mg
Sodium	173 mg
Dietary Fiber	2 g

Also known as rocket, this small, dark-green, slender-leafed vegetable from the Mediterranean is enjoyed for the peppery, slightly bitter flavor. Enjoy it in salads as well as in recipes, such as the one on this page, in which it is used to enhance the flavor of the potatoes.

Arugula is sold in small bunches, often with its stems still attached. Look for smooth, deep-colored leaves free of any brown spots, a sign that the arugula is fresh.

Golden mashed potatoes and arugula

Eating well often means using familiar foods in new ways. In this easy mash, colorful Yukon gold potatoes provide plenty of flavor with little added salt or fat. For a healthful version of a traditional comfort-food dinner, serve this with Baked Vegetable-and-Turkey Loaf (recipe on page 192).

SERVES: 6 | **PREPARATION:** 15 minutes | **COOKING:** 30 minutes

2½ lb (1.25 kg) Yukon gold potatoes, well scrubbed and quartered

1 bunch arugula (rocket), about 4 oz (125 g), stemmed

1 cup (8 fl oz/250 ml) lowfat buttermilk

¼ teaspoon ground pepper

2 tablespoons minced fresh chives

♦ In a large pot fitted with a steamer basket, bring 2 inches (5 cm) water to a boil.

♦ Put the potatoes in the basket. Reduce heat to medium, cover, and steam until the potatoes are very tender, 25–30 minutes.

♦ Cut the arugula leaves crosswise into ¼-inch-thick (6-mm) strips.

♦ In a large bowl, combine the potatoes, buttermilk, and pepper. Using a potato masher, mash to a coarse purée. Stir in the arugula and half the chives.

♦ To serve, divide among individual plates. Top each with an equal amount of the remaining chives.

PER SERVING

Calories	176
Kilojoules	735
Protein	5 g
Carbohydrates	37 g
Total Fat	<1 g
Saturated Fat	<1 g
Cholesterol	3 mg
Sodium	76 mg
Dietary Fiber	3 g

Curried potato skins

Double-panning, the technique of stacking a pan atop a baking sheet to ensure that foods don't burn, guarantees crisp, brown potato skins. Enjoyed as a snack or a side dish, their taste and texture are as satisfying as chips, but with greater nutrient benefit.

SERVES: 6 | **PREPARATION:** 20 minutes | **COOKING:** 1¾ hours

6 large russet potatoes, well scrubbed

1½ tablespoons olive oil

1½ tablespoons water

2 teaspoons curry powder

¼ teaspoon cayenne pepper

½ teaspoon ground pepper

6 green (spring) onions, thinly sliced, including green portions

♦ Preheat an oven to 450°F (230°C).

♦ Prick the potatoes several times with a fork, place directly on the oven rack, and bake until the interior feels soft when squeezed, 65–75 minutes. Cool for 15 minutes.

♦ Line a large, shallow baking pan with aluminum foil, then coat the foil with nonstick cooking spray. Set the prepared pan on a baking sheet.

♦ In a small bowl, stir together the olive oil, water, curry, cayenne, and pepper.

♦ Cut each potato in half lengthwise and scoop out the pulp, leaving a shell of pulp about ¼ inch (6 mm) thick. Reserve the scooped-out potato to make Horseradish Hashed Browns (recipe on page 116).

♦ Using scissors, cut the skins lengthwise into strips about 1 inch (2.5 cm) wide. Place in the prepared baking pan and brush with the olive oil mixture.

♦ Bake for 5 minutes. Scatter the green onions over the top and return to the oven, reversing the position of the baking pan to ensure even baking. Bake until crisp, brown, and sizzling, 8–10 minutes.

♦ To serve, transfer to a platter.

nutrition note

Skins vs. chips

This recipe for Curried Potato Skins is higher in calories than a typical serving of potato chips. But the calories are better for you because more come from carbohydrates. The skins have less fat than the chips and are also higher in dietary fiber.

Compare the nutrients in 1 ounce (30 grams) of potato chips with a single serving of this recipe, noted in the analysis that follows:

POTATO CHIPS

Calories	152
Kilojoules	638
Carbohydrates	15 g
Total Fat	10 g
Saturated Fat	3 g
Cholesterol	0 mg
Sodium	170 mg
Dietary Fiber	1 g

PER SERVING

Calories	220
Kilojoules	922
Protein	5 g
Carbohydrates	42 g
Total Fat	4 g
Saturated Fat	<1 g
Cholesterol	0 mg
Sodium	19 mg
Dietary Fiber	4 g

When available, fresh horseradish adds an extra-special punch to recipes such as this. You'll need to peel and grate the fresh vegetable for use in most recipes. While the fresh provides a more wonderful flavor than prepared, the benefit comes at the price of tears.

Unfortunately, the same essential oils that give horseradish its powerful flavor are released into the air while the root is peeled and grated, causing more irrita-tion to the eyes than onions.

The best way to avoid excessive tears is to try and work in a well-ventilated place and to keep the horseradish at arm's length rather than right under your face. Using good, sharp tools will also reduce some of the wear and tear that helps release the oils into the air. You might also want to try the old-fashioned trick, which is also good for onions, of peeling the root under cold running water to rinse away the vapors before they can reach you.

Horseradish hashed browns

This spicy dish could be called "next-day" potatoes. Use the potato pulp from the Curried Potato Skins (recipe on page 115), cooked the evening before, as the base for this brunch complement, served here with Spicy Spring Greens Salad (recipe on page 43).

SERVES: 4 | **PREPARATION:** 5 minutes | **COOKING:** 15 minutes

4 cups (2 lb/1 kg) baked potato pulp from 6 russet potatoes

1 onion, chopped

1 tablespoon prepared horseradish or freshly grated horseradish

2 teaspoons chopped fresh thyme or 1/2 teaspoon dried thyme

1/2 teaspoon ground pepper

1 teaspoon olive oil

♦ In a large bowl, combine the potato pulp, onion, horseradish, thyme, and pepper.

♦ Coat a 9- or 10-inch (23- or 25-cm) nonstick frying pan with nonstick cooking spray. Place over medium heat and add the olive oil. When hot, add the potato mixture, breaking the large chunks into smaller pieces. Using a spatula, firmly press the potatoes evenly across the bottom of the pan.

♦ Cook until lightly browned on the bottom, 3–4 min-utes. Stir and shake the potatoes to redistribute the mixture, then again press evenly across the bottom of the pan. Cook until browned on the bottom, 3–4 minutes. Stir, shake, then press and pat into a cake for the final time. Cook until well browned and crisp on the bottom, 4–5 minutes.

♦ To serve, invert onto a platter and cut into wedges.

PER SERVING

Calories	175
Kilojoules	734
Protein	4 g
Carbohydrates	38 g
Total Fat	2 g
Saturated Fat	<1 g
Cholesterol	0 mg
Sodium	13 mg
Dietary Fiber	3 g

Oven-fried potato wedges

Malt vinegar is made from malted barley and is a staple condiment most familiarly used for England's fish and chips. It has a robust taste that can stand up to these spiced potato wedges, which make a great snack or a perfect complement to fish dishes. Sprinkle on the vinegar at the table.

SERVES: 6 | **PREPARATION:** 15 minutes | **COOKING:** 30 minutes

2 tablespoons paprika

1/2 teaspoon ground pepper

1/2 teaspoon garlic powder

1/8 teaspoon cayenne pepper

6 russet potatoes, well scrubbed

6 tablespoons (3 fl oz/90 ml) malt vinegar

♦ Preheat an oven to 450°F (230°C). Coat 2 large baking sheets with nonstick cooking spray.

♦ In a large bowl, mix together the paprika, pepper, garlic powder, and cayenne.

♦ Cut the potatoes lengthwise into wedges 1/2–3/4 inch (12 mm–2 cm) thick. Add the potatoes to the spices, tossing to coat well. Arrange the potatoes in single layers on the prepared pans.

♦ Bake for 15 minutes. Turn the potatoes and return to the oven, reversing the position of the baking sheets to ensure even baking. Bake until golden brown and crisp, 10–15 minutes longer.

♦ To serve, transfer to a platter. Pass the malt vinegar at the table.

PER SERVING

Calories	150
Kilojoules	627
Protein	4 g
Carbohydrates	33 g
Total Fat	<1 g
Saturated Fat	0 g
Cholesterol	0 mg
Sodium	14 mg
Dietary Fiber	3 g

Potato salad with Tarragon vinaigrette

Dressed lightly with vinaigrette and fresh herbs, this warm potato salad has fewer calories than the usual mayonnaise-dressed versions. The herb vinaigrette gains body from pectin, a natural product derived from fruit, rather than from a great deal of oil.

SERVES: 6 | **PREPARATION:** 15 minutes | **COOKING:** 45 minutes | **COOLING:** 15 minutes

PER SERVING

Calories	228
Kilojoules	953
Protein	5 g
Carbohydrates	46 g
Total Fat	3 g
Saturated Fat	<1 g
Cholesterol	0 mg
Sodium	155 mg
Dietary Fiber	4 g

Tarragon Vinaigrette (recipe follows)

1 green (spring) onion, thinly sliced, including green portion

3 tablespoons white or red wine vinegar

2 tablespoons chopped fresh tarragon

1/2 teaspoon ground pepper

2 1/2 lb (1.25 kg) red-skinned potatoes, well scrubbed

1/2 lb (250 g) curly endive (chicory/witloof) leaves, chopped

♦ In a large bowl, stir together half the vinaigrette, the green onion, vinegar, tarragon, and pepper.

♦ In a large pot fitted with a steamer basket, bring 2 inches (5 cm) water to a boil. Put the potatoes in the basket. Reduce heat to medium, cover, and steam until just tender, 30–45 minutes.

♦ Cool the potatoes for 15 minutes, then cut them into 1-inch (2.5-cm) chunks, dropping them into the large bowl with the vinaigrette–green onion mixture. Stir and toss to coat the potatoes evenly with the dressing.

♦ To serve, spread the endive on a large platter and drizzle with the remaining vinaigrette. Mound the potato salad in the center.

Tarragon vinaigrette

MAKES: 1 cup (8 fl oz/250 ml) | **PREPARATION:** 5 minutes | **CHILLING:** 1 hour

PER TABLESPOON

Calories	24
Kilojoules	99
Protein	0 g
Carbohydrates	4 g
Total Fat	<1 g
Saturated Fat	<1 g
Cholesterol	0 mg
Sodium	49 mg
Dietary Fiber	0 g

1/3 cup (3 fl oz/80 ml) thawed unsweetened apple juice concentrate

3 tablespoons tarragon vinegar

3 tablespoons water

2 tablespoons powdered pectin

1 tablespoon olive oil

2 tablespoons Dijon mustard

1 tablespoon chopped fresh tarragon

1/4 teaspoon ground pepper

♦ In a small bowl, combine the apple juice, vinegar, water, and pectin. Whisk until the pectin dissolves, about 1 minute. Add the olive oil, mustard, tarragon, and pepper and whisk until blended. Refrigerate in a tightly covered container for at least 1 hour before using; the pectin will cause the dressing to thicken slightly as it chills.

Sweet potato casserole

Pale orange-skinned sweet potatoes cut into chunks and braised with a savory seasoning are a nice change of pace from their candied counterparts. Although often interchangeable, darker-skinned sweet potatoes are not a good substitute in this casserole because they become mushy during braising.

SERVES: 6 | **PREPARATION:** 10 minutes | **COOKING:** 45 minutes

5 sweet potatoes, about
   3 lb (1.5 kg) total

1/2 cup (4 fl oz/125 ml)
   canned vegetable broth

4 drops hot pepper sauce

1/2 teaspoon ground pepper

1 teaspoon dried sage or thyme

6 fresh thyme sprigs

♦ Preheat an oven to 375°F (190°C).

♦ Using a vegetable peeler or paring knife, peel the sweet potatoes. Quarter them lengthwise, then cut them crosswise into chunks about 1 inch (2.5 cm) wide.

♦ Place the sweet potatoes in a 2-qt (2-l) baking dish or casserole. Stir in the broth, hot pepper sauce, pepper, and dried sage or thyme.

♦ Cover with aluminum foil or a lid and bake for 20 minutes, then stir. Cover and continue baking until the potatoes are tender, 20–25 minutes longer.

♦ To serve, divide among individual plates. Top each with a thyme sprig.

PER SERVING

Calories	174
Kilojoules	728
Protein	3 g
Carbohydrates	40 g
Total Fat	<1 g
Saturated Fat	<1 g
Cholesterol	0 mg
Sodium	106 mg
Dietary Fiber	5 g

Cooking pasta

Follow these simple guidelines to make sure your pasta cooks perfectly every time:

- *Use enough water. For every 1 pound (500 grams) of pasta, you need 5–6 quarts (5–6 liters) of water for the pasta to circulate freely and cook evenly.*

- *Use high heat. The water should come to a full, rolling boil before you add the pasta.*

- *Skip the salt. There is no reason to add salt to pasta cooking water except to add unnecessary sodium to the dish.*

- *Don't overcook. Pasta is done when it is tender but still firm to the bite: al dente, as the Italians say. Test at the earliest moment in the manufacturer's suggested cooking time by fishing out a piece or strand with a slotted spoon or long-handled fork; blow briefly to cool the pasta, then bite into it. If the pasta seems hard or still looks white at its center, cook another minute or two before testing again.*

Basil and sun-dried tomato fettuccine

Pasta cooks quickly and lends itself to myriad toppings. Here, the sauce of basil and tomatoes brings the flavors of the Mediterranean to your table in minutes. Pair this complement with a variety of steamed vegetables and a simple green salad for a quick, no-fuss meal.

SERVES: 6 | **PREPARATION:** 15 minutes | **COOKING:** 15 minutes

1/3 cup (3 fl oz/80 ml) canned vegetable broth

1/3 cup (3 fl oz/80 ml) water

6 sun-dried tomatoes (not oil-packed), cut into thin strips

2 teaspoons olive oil

2 garlic cloves, crushed with a garlic press

1/4 teaspoon red pepper flakes

12 oz (375 g) dried fettuccine or linguine

1/2 cup (3/4 oz/20 g) lightly packed torn basil leaves

2 tablespoons grated Parmesan cheese

1 tablespoon dried bread crumbs (see page 79)

◆ In a small saucepan over medium heat, bring the vegetable broth, water, sun-dried tomatoes, olive oil, garlic, and red pepper flakes to a boil. Remove from heat, cover, and keep warm.

◆ Fill a large pot three-quarters full of water and bring to a boil. Add the pasta and cook until al dente, about 10 minutes, or according to package directions. Remove 1/4 cup (2 fl oz/60 ml) of the cooking water, then drain the pasta thoroughly.

◆ In a warmed serving bowl, combine the pasta, broth mixture, basil, and reserved cooking water. Toss to combine and coat the pasta evenly with the sauce.

◆ To serve, divide among individual plates. Top each with an equal amount of the Parmesan and bread crumbs.

PER SERVING

Calories	247
Kilojoules	1,033
Protein	9 g
Carbohydrates	45 g
Total Fat	3 g
Saturated Fat	<1 g
Cholesterol	1 mg
Sodium	103 mg
Dietary Fiber	2 g

Linguine with spicy basil sauce

A dash of red pepper flakes enhances this basil-flavored pasta dish without adding calories or sodium. Vary the flavor of the herb sauce used here and as a topping for the Lentil Soup on page 56 by switching herbs. Oregano and parsley are good options.

SERVES: 6 | **PREPARATION:** 10 minutes | **COOKING:** 10 minutes

³/₄ cup (6 fl oz/180 ml) Green Herb Sauce, made with basil (see page 56)

¹/₄ teaspoon red pepper flakes

12 oz (375 g) dried linguine

1 tablespoon pine nuts, toasted

2 tablespoons grated Parmesan cheese

♦ In a large serving bowl, stir together the herb sauce and pepper flakes.

♦ Fill a large pot three-quarters full of water and bring to a boil. Add the pasta and cook until al dente, about 10 minutes, or according to package directions. Remove ³/₄ cup (6 fl oz/180 ml) of the cooking water, then drain the pasta thoroughly.

♦ To the sauce bowl, add the pasta and reserved cooking water. Toss to combine and coat the pasta evenly with the sauce.

♦ To serve, divide among individual plates. Top each with an equal amount of the pine nuts and Parmesan.

cooking clinic

Toasting nuts and seeds

Although nuts and seeds are high in fat, a little of them goes a long way toward adding crunchy texture and robust flavor to dishes. Enhance their flavor by toasting:

• Spread them in a heavy frying pan in a single layer. Put the pan over low heat and cook the nuts or seeds, stirring constantly, until they take on a golden color and give off a noticeable toasty aroma.

• Toasting time will vary depending on the size of the seeds or nuts. Sesame seeds will toast in less than 1 minute. Pine nuts take 3–4 minutes, while larger nuts can take 5 minutes or longer.

• Always take care to remove the seeds or nuts from the pan as soon as they take on a uniform light golden color. They will continue to darken in color from their residual heat.

PER SERVING

Calories	256
Kilojoules	1,072
Protein	11 g
Carbohydrates	44 g
Total Fat	4 g
Saturated Fat	1 g
Cholesterol	4 mg
Sodium	175 mg
Dietary Fiber	2 g

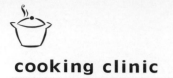

Buying soba

Although Japanese soba is often referred to as buckwheat noodles, it is in fact generally made from a mixture of whole wheat (whole-meal) and buckwheat flours. Pure buckwheat soba is less common.

For an intriguing change of pace, look in well-stocked Asian food stores for soba made with green tea, which gives it a slightly green color and a subtle edge of astringent flavor. Another common type is soba made with Japanese mountain yam, which contributes a pale yellow hue to the noodles.

Curried soba and cucumber relish

Curry powder, used here to enhance a simple dish of Asian buckwheat noodles, is a blend of spices including cumin, coriander, turmeric, ginger, chiles, and pepper. Heating powder in a dry pan causes its flavor to blossom, making it more robust and aromatic.

SERVES: 6 | **PREPARATION:** 25 minutes | **CHILLING:** 1 hour | **COOKING:** 5 minutes

Cucumber Relish

2 cucumbers, peeled

1/4 teaspoon salt

1/3 cup (3 fl oz/80 ml) rice vinegar or cider vinegar

2 tablespoons firmly packed brown sugar

2 teaspoons reduced-sodium soy sauce

1 teaspoon sesame oil

2 1/2 teaspoons curry powder

3/4 cup (6 oz/185 g) plain nonfat yogurt

1/2 cup (3/4 oz/20 g) chopped cilantro (fresh coriander)

1 tablespoon sesame seeds

1/2 teaspoon ground pepper

12 oz (375 g) dried soba noodles

♦ To make the cucumber relish, split the cucumbers in half lengthwise, then cut crosswise into thin slices. In a large bowl, toss the slices with the salt and let stand for 15 minutes. Add the vinegar, brown sugar, soy sauce, and sesame oil to the cucumbers and toss to combine. Cover and refrigerate for 1 hour to allow the flavors to marry before serving.

♦ Put the curry powder in a small, heavy frying pan over medium heat and cook, stirring constantly, until aromatic, about 1 minute. Immediately pour the powder into a large bowl. Stir in the yogurt, cilantro, sesame seeds, and pepper.

♦ Fill a large pot three-quarters full of water and bring to a boil. Add the soba noodles and cook until just tender, about 3 minutes, or according to package directions. Remove 1/3 cup (3 fl oz/80 ml) of the cooking water, then drain the noodles thoroughly.

♦ Add the noodles and reserved cooking water to the curry sauce. Toss to combine and coat the noodles evenly with the sauce.

♦ To serve, divide among individual plates. Top each with an equal amount of the chilled relish. Serve warm or cold.

PER SERVING

Calories	254
Kilojoules	1,063
Protein	11 g
Carbohydrates	52 g
Total Fat	2 g
Saturated Fat	<1 g
Cholesterol	<1 mg
Sodium	640 mg
Dietary Fiber	3 g

Mustard greens and macaroni

Nutrient-rich mustard greens put a new twist on macaroni in this pasta salad combination, which pairs beautifully with a grilled chicken breast for a summer dinner. Toasting sunflower seeds brings out their nutty flavor, without added fat or salt. Try them as a snack.

SERVES: 6 | **PREPARATION:** 15 minutes | **COOKING:** 25 minutes

1 lb (500 g) mustard greens, stemmed and coarsely chopped

3 shallots, minced

1/4 cup (2 fl oz/60 ml) canned vegetable broth

1/4 cup (2 fl oz/60 ml) water

8 oz (250 g) elbow macaroni

1/4 teaspoon hot pepper sauce

1/4 cup (1 1/4 oz/37 g) crumbled soft goat cheese

1 tablespoon sunflower seeds, toasted (see page 127)

6 lime wedges

♦ Coat a 12-inch (30-cm) nonstick frying pan with non-stick cooking spray and place over medium-high heat. When hot, add the mustard greens and shallots and sauté until the greens are partially wilted, 3–5 minutes. Add the broth and water and bring to a boil. Reduce heat to low, cover, and simmer until the greens are tender, 10–12 minutes.

♦ Fill a large pot three-quarters full of water and bring to a boil. Add the pasta and cook until al dente, about 10 minutes, or according to package directions. Remove 1/4 cup (2 fl oz/60 ml) of the cooking water, then drain the pasta thoroughly.

♦ Add the pasta, reserved cooking water, hot pepper sauce, and goat cheese to the greens mixture. Toss to combine and coat the pasta evenly with the sauce.

♦ To serve, divide among individual plates. Top each with an equal amount of the sunflower seeds. Garnish with a lime wedge.

PER SERVING

Calories	187
Kilojoules	781
Protein	8 g
Carbohydrates	33 g
Total Fat	3 g
Saturated Fat	<1 g
Cholesterol	2 mg
Sodium	85 mg
Dietary Fiber	1 g

Orecchiette and capers verde

Orecchiette, or "little ears" in Italian, are roundish, slightly cupped pasta shapes. You can substitute any small pasta shape. Although you can substitute many dried herbs for their fresh counterparts, dill tends to turn bitter when dried. If you can't find fresh dill, use parsley or oregano.

SERVES: 6 | **PREPARATION:** 10 minutes | **COOKING:** 10 minutes

1 tablespoon capers, rinsed, drained, and minced

4 oz (125 g) canned diced mild green chiles

1/2 cup (1/2 oz/15 g) chopped fresh dill

2 garlic cloves, minced

1 tablespoon olive oil

1/2 teaspoon ground pepper

12 oz (375 g) dried orecchiette pasta

♦ In a large bowl, stir in the capers, chiles, dill, garlic, olive oil, and pepper.

♦ Fill a large pot three-quarters full of water and bring to a boil. Add the pasta and cook until al dente, about 10 minutes, or according to package directions. Remove 1/2 cup (4 fl oz/125 ml) of the cooking water, then drain the pasta thoroughly.

♦ Add the pasta and reserved cooking water to the sauce. Toss to combine and coat the pasta evenly with the sauce.

♦ To serve, divide among individual plates.

PER SERVING

Calories	239
Kilojoules	1,003
Protein	8 g
Carbohydrates	44 g
Total Fat	3 g
Saturated Fat	<1 g
Cholesterol	0 mg
Sodium	184 mg
Dietary Fiber	2 g

Gingered spring peas and fusilli

Sugar snap peas look like shelling peas but are smaller and have completely edible pods. Snow peas are long and flat and contain tiny lentil-sized peas. Use either of these spring favorites in this quick and colorful concoction. Just trim off the tough ends and any strings, leaving the pods whole.

SERVES: 6 | **PREPARATION:** 20 minutes | **COOKING:** 10 minutes

2 cucumbers, peeled

1/4 teaspoon salt

3/4 lb (375 g) sugar snap peas or snow peas (mangetouts)

12 oz (375 g) dried fusilli pasta

Tarragon Vinaigrette (recipe on page 120)

1/2 cup (3/4 oz/20 g) chopped cilantro (fresh coriander)

1/2 cup (3/4 oz/20 g) chopped fresh flat-leaf (Italian) parsley

2 tablespoons grated fresh ginger

2 garlic cloves, minced

1/2 teaspoon ground pepper

◆ Halve the cucumbers lengthwise and scrape the seeds from the center. Cut crosswise into 1/4-inch (6-mm) slices and place in a colander. Sprinkle with the salt, toss to combine, and let stand 15 minutes to drain.

◆ Fill a large pot three-quarters full of water and bring to a boil.

◆ Put the peas in a large metal strainer and lower them into the boiling water. Blanch sugar snap peas for 1 minute, snow peas for 30 seconds. Rinse under cold water and pat dry.

◆ Add the pasta to the boiling water and cook until al dente, 8–10 minutes, or according to package directions. Rinse under cold water and drain thoroughly.

◆ In a large bowl, whisk together the vinaigrette, cilantro, parsley, ginger, garlic, and pepper. Stir in the cucumbers and peas.

◆ To the large bowl, add the pasta. Toss gently to combine and coat the pasta evenly with the dressing.

◆ To serve, divide among individual plates. Serve as soon as possible. Once refrigerated, this pasta never regains its freshly cooked taste or texture.

cooking clinic

Grating ginger

The tropical ginger plant yields a sweet, strong, warm-tasting spice that enhances savory and sweet recipes alike. You can find whole fresh ginger rhizomes, which are commonly but incorrectly called ginger roots, in the vegetable section of most food stores or in Asian markets, produce shops, or farmers' markets.

• *Before slicing, chopping, or grating fresh ginger, use a small, sharp knife to peel away the brown, papery skin from only the part of the rhizome you will be using.*

• *To grate the ginger, rub it against the fine holes of a small handheld grater. If you plan to use ginger frequently, you might also visit an Asian market to search out a special ginger grater, a small ceramic device whose sharp little rasps very efficiently break up the rhizome's fibrous flesh.*

• *You can also squeeze small chunks of peeled ginger through a garlic press to make a pulp.*

PER SERVING

Calories	314
Kilojoules	1,313
Protein	9 g
Carbohydrates	60 g
Total Fat	3 g
Saturated Fat	<1 g
Cholesterol	0 mg
Sodium	333 mg
Dietary Fiber	4 g

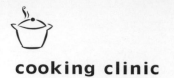

A guide to tiny pastas

If you can't find orzo or want to try a variation on this recipe, keep an eye open for one of these classic tiny pastas listed here or larger shapes on page 171.

Acini di Pepe. *"Peppercorns"*

Alphabet. *Assorted letter shapes*

Anellini. *Small rings*

Conchigliette Picole. *"Little shells"*

Farfalline. *"Little butterflies"*

Risi. *"Rice," similar to orzo*

Seme di Melone. *"Melon seeds," resembling flattened orzo*

Stellette. *"Little stars"*

Stelline. *"Little stars"*

Tubettini. *"Tiny tubes"*

Orzo, pea, and pepper salad

Orzo, a rice-shaped pasta, absorbs the dark, fragrant balsamic vinegar dressing in this colorful salad. You can make this dish up to 2 days before serving. It travels well, too, making it an excellent choice for a picnic or other al fresco meal.

SERVES: 6 | **PREPARATION:** 15 minutes | **COOKING:** 10 minutes

3 tablespoons balsamic vinegar

1½ tablespoons water

2 teaspoons olive oil

1½ teaspoons Dijon mustard

1 garlic clove, crushed with a garlic press

¼ teaspoon pepper

3 green (spring) onions, thinly sliced, including green portions

1 red bell pepper (capsicum), seeded, stemmed, and cut into ½-inch (12-mm) squares

10 oz (315 g) orzo pasta

1 cup (5 oz/155 g) frozen peas

♦ In a large bowl, whisk together the balsamic vinegar, water, olive oil, mustard, garlic, and pepper until well blended. Stir in the green onions and bell pepper.

♦ Fill a large pot three-quarters full of water and bring to a boil. Add the pasta and cook for 6 minutes. Add the peas and cook until the pasta is al dente and peas are tender-crisp, 2–3 minutes. Drain thoroughly.

♦ To the large bowl, add the orzo and peas. Toss gently to combine and coat the pasta evenly with the dressing. Cool to room temperature, stirring occasionally. If made in advance, refrigerate in a tightly covered container for up to 2 days.

♦ To serve, divide among individual plates.

PER SERVING

Calories	217
Kilojoules	908
Protein	8 g
Carbohydrates	41 g
Total Fat	2 g
Saturated Fat	<1 g
Cholesterol	0 mg
Sodium	36 mg
Dietary Fiber	2 g

When you think of dining as a form of entertainment, consider entrees as the featured players. On the pages that follow, you'll find example after example of recipes that give star status to eating well. These entrees have subtle differences that distinguish them from traditional main-course offerings. As a balanced part of eating well, these recipes cleverly incorporate generous amounts of vegetables, fruits, legumes, and grains, and keep amounts of animal foods to recommended serving sizes. Many are dynamic combinations of rices, pastas, beans, and vegetables cooked without meat. Of course, there are many familiar choices as well, featuring chicken, turkey, fish, shellfish, lamb, pork, and beef. As varied and delicious as these entrees are, they share another common trait besides their healthful attributes: All are worthy of grabbing the spotlight on your dining table.

entrees

Vegetable and wheat berry casserole

Robust and satisfying, this entree counterpoints the chewy, nutlike taste of wheat berries with an oven-baked medley of summer vegetables reminiscent of French ratatouille. Feel free to stir in other fresh herbs, such as basil or chives, along with the parsley before serving.

SERVES: 6 | **PREPARATION:** 25 minutes | **COOKING:** 1^1/$_2$ hours

2^1/$_8$ cups (1 lb/500 g) wheat berries

12 cups (96 fl oz/3 l) water

2 lb (1 kg) eggplant (aubergine), cut into ^{1}/$_2$-inch (12-mm) cubes

28 oz (875 g) canned diced tomatoes

4 zucchini (courgettes), cut crosswise into ^{1}/$_2$-inch-thick (12-mm) slices

2 onions, cut into ^{1}/$_2$-inch-thick (12-mm) slices and separated into rings

1 green bell pepper (capsicum), stemmed, seeded, and cut into ^{3}/$_4$-inch (2-cm) squares

1 red bell pepper (capsicum), stemmed, seeded, and cut into ^{3}/$_4$-inch (2-cm) squares

^{1}/$_4$ cup (1 oz/30 g) canned pitted olives, drained and sliced

4 garlic cloves, minced

^{1}/$_4$ teaspoon cayenne pepper

^{1}/$_4$ cup (^{1}/$_3$ oz/10 g) chopped fresh flat-leaf (Italian) parsley

2 tablespoons red wine vinegar

6 fresh flat-leaf (Italian) parsley sprigs

◆ In a large pot, combine the wheat berries and water. Bring to a boil, reduce heat to low, cover, and simmer until most of the water has been absorbed and the wheat berries are chewy and tender, about 1^1/$_2$ hours. Drain.

◆ Meanwhile, preheat an oven to 400°F (200°C).

◆ In a large ovenproof casserole or roasting pan, combine the eggplant, tomatoes and their juice, zucchini, onions, bell peppers, olives, garlic, and cayenne. Mix thoroughly. Cover and bake, stirring once or twice, until the vegetables are tender, about 1 hour.

◆ To serve, stir the chopped parsley and vinegar into the vegetables. Divide the wheat berries among individual plates. Top each with an equal amount of the vegetables. Garnish with a parsley sprig.

Hearty grain-filled peppers

Enjoy the homey goodness of meatless stuffed bell peppers, which are filled in this recipe with a robust lowfat combination of cracked wheat, mushrooms, tomatoes, onions, and garlic. Complement them with a refreshing vegetable such as the Cucumber Relish shown here (recipe on page 128).

SERVES: 6 | **PREPARATION:** 25 minutes | **COOKING:** 1 hour

4 cups (32 fl oz/1 l) water

1/2 teaspoon ground cinnamon

1/2 teaspoon ground cumin

2 cups (12 oz/375 g) bulgur wheat

8 oz (250 g) white mushrooms, coarsely chopped

1 1/2 cups (9 oz/280 g) diced fresh tomatoes or 14 1/2 oz (455 g) canned diced tomatoes, drained

1 onion, finely chopped

2 garlic cloves, minced

1/2 cup (1/2 oz/15 g) chopped fresh flat-leaf (Italian) parsley

1/3 cup (2 oz/60 g) raisins

3 red bell peppers (capsicums), halved, stemmed, and seeded

3 green bell peppers (capsicums), halved, stemmed, and seeded

6 tablespoons (3 oz/90 g) plain nonfat yogurt

1 tablespoon sunflower seeds, toasted (see page 127)

◆ In a large saucepan, bring the water, cinnamon, and cumin to a boil. Stir in the bulgur. When the water returns to a boil, reduce heat to low. Cover and simmer until the water is absorbed, about 15 minutes.

◆ In a large frying pan over medium heat, combine the mushrooms, tomatoes, onion, garlic, and parsley. Cover and cook, stirring occasionally, until the vegetables are tender but not mushy, about 10 minutes.

◆ Stir the mushroom mixture and raisins into the cooked bulgur.

◆ Preheat an oven to 400°F (200°C). Coat a shallow baking dish with nonstick cooking spray.

◆ Arrange the bell pepper halves in a single layer, cut side up, in the prepared pan. Divide the bulgur mixture equally among the bell peppers, mounding slightly. Cover tightly with aluminum foil and bake until the peppers are tender and the filling is heated through, about 45 minutes.

◆ To serve, place 2 bell pepper halves on individual plates. Top each with 1/2 tablespoon of the yogurt. Garnish with the sunflower seeds.

nutrition note

Bulgur

Bulgur is wheat that has been steamed and dried, then cracked into fine, medium, or coarse particles. The medium or coarse grinds are best suited for grain dishes such as the one on this page or for salads; finely ground bulgur is better suited for use in baked goods and desserts.

Not all varieties of bulgur, however, are whole wheat. When shopping for the grain, check the ingredient list or the granules to see if the dark-brown bran is present.

Like other whole grains, whole wheat bulgur retains the fiber and more vitamins and minerals that are stored in the kernel's bran and germ.

PER SERVING

Calories	292
Kilojoules	1,223
Protein	11 g
Carbohydrates	63 g
Total Fat	2 g
Saturated Fat	<1 g
Cholesterol	<1 mg
Sodium	126 mg
Dietary Fiber	14 g

Thai-style mushroom and tofu stir-fry

In this dish, the rich textures of mushrooms and tofu are highlighted by the savory flavors of peanut butter and sesame oil. Joined with crisp snow peas and water chestnuts, they make a hearty Asian-inspired main dish. Serve with steamed brown or white rice.

SERVES: 6 | **PREPARATION:** 25 minutes | **COOKING:** 10 minutes

1/4 cup (2 oz/60 g) creamy reduced-fat peanut butter

2 tablespoons reduced-sodium soy sauce

2 tablespoons lime juice

1/3 cup (3 fl oz/80 ml) water

2 teaspoons sesame oil

2 teaspoons cornstarch (cornflour)

1/2 teaspoon red pepper flakes

12 oz (375 g) oyster mushrooms, sliced

1/2 lb (250 g) snow peas (mangetouts), ends trimmed and strings pulled

8 oz (250 g) canned sliced water chestnuts, rinsed and drained

1 lb (500 g) firm tofu, cut into 1/2-inch (12-mm) cubes

1/2 cup (2/3 oz/20 g) chopped cilantro (fresh coriander)

♦ In a small bowl, whisk together the peanut butter, soy sauce, and lime juice until smooth. Add the water, sesame oil, cornstarch, and pepper flakes and whisk until blended.

♦ Coat a nonstick wok or a large nonstick frying pan with nonstick cooking spray and heat over high heat. Add the mushrooms and stir-fry until lightly browned, about 4 minutes. Add the snow peas and continue stir-frying until the peas are tender-crisp, 2–3 minutes.

♦ Add the peanut butter mixture, water chestnuts, and tofu and stir-fry until the sauce thickens slightly, about 1 minute.

♦ To serve, transfer to a bowl. Sprinkle with the cilantro.

Curried vegetables with Mango chutney

Experienced cooks add their curry powder to an onion while it sautées. The heat causes the curry flavor to blossom, opening up like a flower. Serve this Indian-inspired dish with brown rice (see page 107) and Mango Chutney, using either a commercial version or the recipe below.

SERVES: 6 | **PREPARATION:** 25 minutes | **COOKING:** 30 minutes

1 tablespoon canola oil

1 onion, chopped

1 tablespoon curry powder

1 butternut squash, about 1 lb (500 g), peeled, seeded, and cut into cubes

2 rutabagas, cut into cubes

3 carrots, halved lengthwise and cut into pieces

2 cups (16 fl oz/500 ml) water

1 cup (8 fl oz/250 ml) canned vegetable broth

1/2 teaspoon dried thyme

1/2 teaspoon ground pepper

1 lb (500 g) broccoli, cut into florets

6 tablespoons Mango Chutney (recipe follows)

♦ In a large saucepan over medium heat, heat the oil. Add the onion and curry powder and sauté until the onion is soft, about 5 minutes.

♦ Stir in the squash, rutabagas, carrots, water, broth, thyme, and pepper. Increase heat to high and bring to a boil. Reduce heat to low, cover, and simmer for 10 minutes.

♦ Stir in the broccoli, cover, and simmer until the vegetables are tender, 10–12 minutes.

♦ To serve, mound in a large, shallow bowl. Accompany with the chutney.

PER SERVING

Calories	162
Kilojoules	679
Protein	6 g
Carbohydrates	33 g
Total Fat	3 g
Saturated Fat	<1 g
Cholesterol	0 mg
Sodium	226 mg
Dietary Fiber	7 g

Mango chutney

MAKES: 2 cups (20 oz/625 g) | **PREPARATION:** 10 minutes | **COOKING:** 20 minutes

2 mangoes

1/2 cup (3 1/2 oz/105 g) firmly packed brown sugar

1/2 cup (4 fl oz/125 ml) cider vinegar

1/2 cup (3 oz/90 g) raisins

1 tablespoon fresh grated ginger or 1 teaspoon ground ginger

1/8 teaspoon ground cinnamon

1/4 teaspoon ground allspice

♦ Peel and pit the mangoes and cut the flesh into cubes. In a large saucepan, bring the mangoes, brown sugar, vinegar, raisins, ginger, cinnamon, and allspice to a boil. Reduce heat to low and simmer, stirring occasionally, until the mangoes are very tender and the mixture has thickened slightly, 15–20 minutes.

♦ Cool to room temperature. Serve now, or refrigerate in a tightly covered container for up to 4 days.

PER TABLESPOON

Calories	30
Kilojoules	125
Protein	<1 g
Carbohydrates	8 g
Total Fat	<1 g
Saturated Fat	0 g
Cholesterol	0 mg
Sodium	2 mg
Dietary Fiber	<1 g

cooking clinic

Choosing parsnips

When buying parsnips, look for smooth well-shaped cream- or tan-colored small to medium roots. The longer the root and the broader its stem end, the woodier and coarser it will be.

Keep parsnips cold in the refrigerator. During storage, some of their starch will change to sugar, producing a sweeter flavor. In general, the longer a parsnip has been stored, the sweeter it will taste. Maximum sweetness develops in about 2 weeks.

Roasted winter vegetables

Hearty and heart-healthy, this vegetable array makes a warming and filling main course for a cold winter night. Highlight its earthy flavors with a zesty green vegetable such as Broccoli in Spicy Orange Sauce, shown here (recipe on page 96).

SERVES: 6 | **PREPARATION:** 15 minutes | **COOKING:** 45 minutes

- 1 butternut squash, 1 lb (500 g), peeled, seeded, and cut into cubes
- 3 red-skinned potatoes, cut into cubes
- 2 turnips, peeled and cut into cubes
- 3 carrots, halved lengthwise and cut into pieces
- 3 parsnips, halved lengthwise and cut into pieces
- 1 tablespoon olive oil
- 2 teaspoons dried thyme
- 1/2 teaspoon ground pepper
- 3 tablespoons malt vinegar
- 2 tablespoons chopped fresh flat-leaf (Italian) parsley
- 2 garlic cloves, minced

♦ Preheat an oven to 425°F (220°C). Coat a large roasting pan with nonstick cooking spray.

♦ Put the squash, potatoes, turnips, carrots, and parsnips in the pan. Add the oil, thyme, and pepper and stir and toss to combine and coat the vegetables evenly.

♦ Roast, stirring occasionally, until the vegetables are lightly browned and tender when pierced, about 45 minutes.

♦ In a large bowl, stir together the vinegar, parsley, and garlic. Add the vegetables and toss to combine.

♦ To serve, divide among individual plates.

PER SERVING

Calories	194
Kilojoules	813
Protein	4 g
Carbohydrates	40 g
Total Fat	3 g
Saturated Fat	<1 g
Cholesterol	0 mg
Sodium	56 mg
Dietary Fiber	7 g

Cruciferous stir-fry over rice

Two nutrient-rich vegetables, broccoli and cauliflower, are combined here in an Asian-style stir-fry. Serve the colorful stir-fry with an aromatic long-grained rice, which makes this easy meal particularly memorable.

SERVES: 6 | **PREPARATION:** 20 minutes | **COOKING:** 20 minutes

3½ cups (28 fl oz/875 ml) water

1 cup (8 fl oz/250 ml) canned vegetable broth

2 tablespoons grated orange zest

1½ teaspoons five-spice powder

3 cups (21 oz/655 g) basmati or Texmati rice

1 tablespoon canola oil

1 tablespoon minced fresh ginger

3 garlic cloves, minced

4 green (spring) onions, finely chopped, including green portions

¼ teaspoon red pepper flakes

1 lb (500 g) broccoli, cut into florets

1 lb (500 g) cauliflower, cut into florets

8 oz (250 g) firm tofu, drained, blotted dry, and cut into ½-inch (12-mm) cubes

8 oz (250 g) oyster mushrooms, halved

1 tablespoon sesame seeds

1 tablespoon reduced-sodium soy sauce

♦ In a large, heavy saucepan, bring the water, broth, orange zest, and five-spice powder to a boil. Stir in the rice. When the liquid returns to a boil, cover and reduce heat to low. Simmer until the rice is tender and the liquid has been absorbed, about 18 minutes.

♦ Remove the pan from heat and let stand 5 minutes, covered, then fluff the rice with a fork.

♦ Meanwhile, in a wok or large nonstick frying pan over high heat, heat half the oil. Add half each of the ginger, garlic, green onions, and pepper flakes, and stir-fry until fragrant, about 30 seconds. Add half the broccoli and cauliflower and stir-fry until the broccoli turns bright green, about 2 minutes.

♦ Add half the tofu, mushrooms, sesame seeds, and soy sauce, and stir-fry until the tofu is heated through and the vegetables are tender-crisp, 2–3 minutes. Transfer the mixture to a large bowl and keep warm. Repeat with the remaining ingredients.

♦ To serve, divide the rice among individual plates. Top each with an equal amount of the vegetables and tofu.

nutrition note

Rice

There are many different varieties of rice, but the long and short of it is they can all be divided into two categories, short and long.

Short- to medium-grained types cook to a sticky or creamy consistency, such as Japanese sticky rice and the Arborio variety used in Italian risotto.

Long-grain rices cook to a fluffy consistency with separate grains, such as the fragrant Indian basmati and American-grown Texmati varieties.

All rices are high in complex carbohydrates. White rice is grain from which the bran has been stripped away, along with much of its fiber and nutrients.

Brown rice, which still has the bran, is higher in fiber than white rice. White rice labeled "enriched" has had several nutrients added back to a level comparable to the unrefined grain, but it is still lower in fiber.

PER SERVING

Calories	480
Kilojoules	2,007
Protein	22 g
Carbohydrates	91 g
Total Fat	9 g
Saturated Fat	<1 g
Cholesterol	0 mg
Sodium	352 mg
Dietary Fiber	6 g

Cleaning leeks

With their mild, sweet, oniony flavor, leeks make a wonderful addition to savory dishes.

Because they are grown in sandy soil, leeks tend to trap grit between their multilayered leaves and must be washed thoroughly before cooking.

• *To wash a leek, simply slit it lengthwise, starting at the point where the white base meets the green and continuing through the leafy tops.*

• *Swish the leek back and forth in a basin of water, or rinse under cold running water, until no grit remains between the leaves.*

• *Pat dry, trim the leek, and slice as directed in the recipe.*

Summer savory spinach frittata

An open-faced omelet is a wonderful opportunity to try cholesterol-free pasteurized egg product in place of 6 eggs. Either 5 cups (5 oz/155 g) of fresh spinach leaves, steamed, or 10 oz (315 g) frozen spinach, thawed, will yield the right amount of vegetable.

SERVES: 6 | **PREPARATION:** 15 minutes | **COOKING:** 20 minutes

1½ cups (12 fl oz/375 ml) pasteurized egg product

2 tablespoons chopped fresh summer savory or 2 teaspoons dried summer savory

1 tablespoon water

1 tablespoon olive oil

1 cup (8 oz/250 g) cooked, chopped spinach

2 leeks, thinly sliced, including green portions

¾ cup (3½ oz/105 g) cooked peas or thawed frozen peas

½ teaspoon ground pepper

¼ cup (1 oz/30 g) grated Gruyère or Swiss cheese

¼ cup (1 oz/30 g) finely diced yellow or red bell pepper (capsicum)

♦ In a bowl, whisk together the egg product, summer savory, and water.

♦ In a large nonstick frying pan over medium heat, heat the oil. Add the spinach, leeks, peas, and pepper. Cook, stirring frequently, until the leeks are tender, about 10 minutes. Transfer to a bowl.

♦ To prevent the mixture from sticking, wipe the frying pan clean, then coat it with nonstick cooking spray. Return to medium heat. Put the vegetables back in the pan and pat them into an even layer. Pour in the egg mixture; don't worry if it doesn't quite cover the vegetables. Cook, shaking the pan occasionally to keep the frittata from sticking, until the eggs are set around the edges but soft and runny in the center, about 3 minutes.

♦ Sprinkle with the cheese and bell pepper. Cover and cook, continuing to shake the frying pan occasionally, until the eggs are completely set and the cheese is melted, about 3 minutes longer.

♦ To serve, cut into wedges. Serve hot, warm, or cold.

PER SERVING

Calories	134
Kilojoules	560
Protein	11 g
Carbohydrates	14 g
Total Fat	4 g
Saturated Fat	1 g
Cholesterol	5 mg
Sodium	155 mg
Dietary Fiber	2 g

Roasted vegetable fajitas

The Spanish word fajita, *meaning little bands or sashes, refers to the strips of skirt steak for which the dish was first developed by a butcher in Austin, Texas, in the 1960s. Today, the term applies to any strips of savory food cooked to flavorful intensity, such as these aromatic summer vegetables.*

SERVES: 6 | **PREPARATION:** 25 minutes | **COOKING:** 30 minutes

1 small eggplant (aubergine),
1 lb (500 g), cut into
1/2-inch (12-mm) dice

1 tablespoon canola oil

2 zucchini (courgettes), halved
lengthwise and cut into
thin slices

1 red bell pepper (capsicum),
stemmed, seeded, and cut
into thin strips

1 green bell pepper (capsicum),
stemmed, seeded, and cut
into thin strips

1 red (Spanish) onion, cut
into 1/2-inch-thick
(12-mm) slices

1 tablespoon balsamic vinegar

2 garlic cloves, minced

12 whole wheat (wholemeal)
tortillas, 8 inches (20 cm)
in diameter

4 cups (28 oz/875 g) cooked,
warm brown rice (see
page 107)

6 tablespoons Fresh Tomato
Salsa (recipe on page 99)

12 cilantro (fresh coriander)
sprigs

♦ Preheat an oven to 450°F (230°C). Coat a baking pan with nonstick cooking spray.

♦ In a large bowl, toss the eggplant with the oil to coat. Add the zucchini, bell peppers, onion, vinegar, and garlic, tossing to mix well. Transfer the mixture to the prepared pan. Roast, uncovered, stirring once or twice, until the vegetables are tender, 25–30 minutes.

♦ Heat a dry large frying pan (not one with a nonstick surface) over medium heat. One at a time, heat the tortillas in the hot pan on each side until softened, about 20 seconds per side.

♦ To serve, divide the tortillas among individual plates. Spread an equal amount of the vegetable mixture and rice on each tortilla. Top with 1/2 tablespoon of the salsa. Fold in both sides of each tortilla up over the filling, then roll to close. Garnish with the cilantro sprigs.

cooking clinic

Choosing tortillas

The traditional unleavened bread wrappers of Mexico, tortillas are a versatile way to add grains to your day. Tortillas divide into two basic categories: corn and wheat. Wheat tortillas made from white flour are often labled as flour. Whole-wheat tortillas are made from the whole grain flour.

PER SERVING

Calories	369
Kilojoules	1,545
Protein	11 g
Carbohydrates	70 g
Total Fat	6 g
Saturated Fat	<1 g
Cholesterol	0 mg
Sodium	310 mg
Dietary Fiber	9 g

PER SERVING

Calories	455
Kilojoules	1,904
Protein	12 g
Carbohydrates	95 g
Total Fat	3 g
Saturated Fat	<1 g
Cholesterol	2 mg
Sodium	87 mg
Dietary Fiber	7 g

Tandoori sweet potatoes and rice

The baked sweet potatoes in this recipe are rubbed with a marinade similar to that used for tandoori chicken, a traditional roasted Indian dish. Cucumber-yogurt sauce, known in India as raita, *makes a cool companion. Serve with steamed brown rice.*

SERVES: 6 | **PREPARATION:** 25 minutes | **MARINATING:** 30 minutes | **COOKING:** 45 minutes

Sauce

1 cucumber, 12 oz (375 g), peeled, halved, seeded, and sliced

1 cup (8 oz/250 g) plain nonfat yogurt

1/2 cup (3/4 oz/20 g) chopped fresh mint

1 teaspoon sugar

1/4 teaspoon ground pepper

Marinade

1 cup (8 oz/250 g) plain nonfat yogurt

3 tablespoons lemon juice

2 teaspoons olive oil

3 garlic cloves, minced

1 tablespoon grated fresh ginger

4 teaspoons curry powder

1/2 teaspoon cayenne pepper

3 large sweet potatoes, peeled and cut into 1-inch-thick (2.5-cm) slices

6 cups (30 oz/940 g) cooked, hot brown rice (see page 107)

2 tablespoons chopped fresh sage or 2 teaspoons dried sage

♦ To make the sauce, in a medium bowl, stir together the cucumber, yogurt, mint, sugar, and pepper. Cover and refrigerate for at least 3 hours or up to 24 hours.

♦ To make the marinade, in a large nonreactive bowl, combine the yogurt, lemon juice, olive oil, garlic, ginger, curry powder, and cayenne.

♦ Using a sharp knife, score the surface of the sweet potatoes in a crisscross pattern about 1/4 inch (6 mm) deep at 1-inch (2.5-cm) intervals. Add to the bowl with the marinade and toss to coat. Marinate at room temperature for 30 minutes, tossing once after 15 minutes.

♦ Preheat an oven to 400°F (200°C). Coat a large, shallow nonreactive baking pan with nonstick cooking spray.

♦ Reserving the marinade, arrange the sweet potato slices in a single layer in the prepared pan. Bake, brushing with the reserved marinade every 15 minutes, until the potatoes are tender, about 45 minutes.

♦ To serve, toss the rice with the sage. Divide the rice, sweet potato slices, and sauce among individual plates.

Quick baked beans with Carrot relish

Enjoy all the rich-tasting, aromatic pleasures of a bean pot that has baked for hours, in just a fraction of the time. Canned beans, or your own precooked legumes, make this satisfying recipe incredibly easy. The simple Carrot Relish that accompanies it adds color.

SERVES: 8 | **PREPARATION:** 30 minutes | **COOKING:** 40 minutes

2 cups (16 fl oz/500 ml) apple juice

2/3 cup (5 fl oz/160 ml) tomato juice

1/3 cup (4 oz/125 g) molasses

3 tablespoons brown sugar

1 large onion, chopped

2 teaspoons mustard powder

1 tablespoon grated fresh ginger

8 cups (3 1/2 lb/1.75 kg) cooked pinto beans (see page 160) or canned pinto beans, rinsed and drained

1 cup (5 oz/155 g) Carrot Relish (recipe follows)

◆ In a 4-qt (4-l) saucepan or dutch oven over high heat, bring the apple juice, tomato juice, molasses, brown sugar, onion, mustard, and ginger to a boil. Add the beans and return to a boil. Reduce heat to medium-low, cover, and cook, stirring occasionally, for 20 minutes.

◆ Remove the cover and continue to cook, stirring occasionally, until the liquid is thick and coats the beans lightly, about 20 minutes.

◆ To serve, divide among individual soup plates. Top each with 2 tablespoons of the Carrot Relish.

PER SERVING

Calories	386
Kilojoules	1,617
Protein	17 g
Carbohydrates	79 g
Total Fat	1 g
Saturated Fat	<1 g
Cholesterol	0 mg
Sodium	128 mg
Dietary Fiber	9 g

Carrot relish

MAKES: 3 cups (15 oz/470 g) | **PREPARATION:** 15 minutes | **COOKING:** 5 minutes | **CHILLING:** 2 hours

1 lb (500 g) carrots, diced

1/4 cup (1 oz/30 g) chopped red (Spanish) onion

1/4 cup (1 oz/30 g) chopped green bell pepper (capsicum)

1/4 cup (2 fl oz/60 ml) tomato purée

1/4 cup (2 fl oz/60 ml) cider vinegar

1 tablespoon sugar

1/4 teaspoon salt

1/4 teaspoon ground pepper

◆ In a large pot fitted with a steamer basket, bring 2 inches (5 cm) water to a boil. Add the carrots to the basket, cover, reduce heat to a simmer, and steam until the carrots are tender-crisp, about 5 minutes.

◆ In a bowl, stir and toss together the carrots, onion, bell pepper, tomato purée, vinegar, sugar, salt, and pepper. Cover and refrigerate for at least 2 hours or up to 2 days.

PER TABLESPOON

Calories	11
Kilojoules	48
Protein	<1 g
Carbohydrates	3 g
Total Fat	<1 g
Saturated Fat	0 g
Cholesterol	0 mg
Sodium	40 mg
Dietary Fiber	1 g

Cooking beans

For convenience, canned beans can be used as indicated in the recipes in this book. Be sure to rinse and drain canned beans before measuring.

To cook dried beans, first sort through them to remove any stones, fibers, or misshapen or discolored items. Rinse under cold water.

To rehydrate them for even cooking, presoak beans and other large dried legumes, such as chickpeas (garbanzo beans) and black-eyed peas, in cold water to cover. Soak for 3 hours or up to overnight. To presoak faster, bring the beans to a simmer, remove from heat, cover, and let stand for 1–1½ hours before draining.

To neutralize natural substances that would otherwise cause gas, boil the beans in water to cover for 10–15 minutes. Then, reduce heat and simmer until the beans are tender, 30 minutes to 1 hour, or more, depending on the variety and age of the beans.

PER SERVING

Calories	273
Kilojoules	1,142
Protein	10 g
Carbohydrates	53 g
Total Fat	3 g
Saturated Fat	<1 g
Cholesterol	0 mg
Sodium	208 mg
Dietary Fiber	5 g

Pinto bean and vegetable stir-fry

The secret to success with this recipe lies in using rice that you have precooked and chilled in the refrigerator until firm. Cooked, cold rice withstands the heat and stirring of a second cooking far better than freshly cooked rice, which would break apart and turn mushy.

SERVES: 6 | **PREPARATION:** 15 minutes | **COOKING:** 10 minutes

2 cups (10 oz/315 g) cooked, cold long-grain brown or white rice (see page 107)

2 cups (10 oz/315 g) cooked, cold wild rice (see page 180)

2 cups (14 oz/440 g) cooked or canned pinto beans, rinsed and drained

1 tablespoon canola oil

2 pattypan squashes, cut into quarters

1 green bell pepper (capsicum), stemmed, seeded, and thinly sliced

1 red bell pepper (capsicum), stemmed, seeded, and thinly sliced

2 tablespoons reduced-sodium soy sauce

2 green (spring) onions, thinly sliced, including green portions

½ cup (3 oz/90 g) dried currants

½ teaspoon ground pepper

♦ In a large bowl, combine the long-grain and wild rices, breaking apart any lumps. If using canned beans, place in a colander and rinse under cold running water, then drain thoroughly.

♦ In a large frying pan or wok over high heat, heat the oil. Add the squashes and bell peppers and sauté until softened, 4–5 minutes.

♦ Reduce heat to medium and add the rice and beans. Cook, stirring frequently, until heated through, about 5 minutes. Add the soy sauce, green onions, currants, and pepper and stir to combine.

♦ To serve, divide among individual plates.

Parsnip, potato, and lima bean hash

The word "hash" comes from the French hacher, *meaning to chop up. Just as cream does in diner-style hashes, the sugars naturally present in the nonfat evaporated milk develop a rich-tasting, well-browned crust on this savory mixture of root vegetables and legumes.*

SERVES: 6 | **PREPARATION:** 15 minutes | **COOKING:** 1¼ hours

4 red-skinned potatoes,
   1¼ lb (625 g) total

2 parsnips, peeled

2 teaspoons olive oil

1 onion, chopped

2 celery stalks, thinly sliced

3½ cups (20 oz/625 g)
   frozen lima beans, thawed

2 tablespoons chopped fresh
   thyme or 2 teaspoons
   dried thyme

½ teaspoon ground pepper

⅔ cup (5 fl oz/160 ml)
   nonfat evaporated milk

♦ In a large pot fitted with a steamer basket, bring 2 inches (5 cm) of water to a boil. Put the potatoes in the basket, cover, and steam for 20 minutes. Add the parsnips to the basket and continue to steam until both vegetables are tender, 25 minutes longer.

♦ Cool the potatoes and parsnips to room temperature, then cut each into ½-inch (12-mm) cubes.

♦ Coat a nonstick frying pan with nonstick cooking spray. Place over medium heat and add the olive oil. When hot, add the onion and celery and sauté until soft, about 5 minutes.

♦ Stir in the potatoes, parsnips, beans, thyme, and pepper. Using a spatula, press the hash down firmly and evenly. Cook, shaking occasionally, until lightly browned on the bottom, 5–7 minutes.

♦ Pour in half the milk and stir the hash, mixing some of the browned bottom crust into the hash. Press down firmly and cook until browned on the bottom, about 5 minutes. Stir in the remaining milk, press down a final time, and cook, shaking occasionally, until the hash is quite brown on the bottom, about 5 minutes longer.

♦ To serve, cut into wedges and place on individual plates. For a more striking presentation, invert onto a large platter.

PER SERVING

Calories	257
Kilojoules	1,077
Protein	11 g
Carbohydrates	49 g
Total Fat	2 g
Saturated Fat	<1 g
Cholesterol	1 mg
Sodium	111 mg
Dietary Fiber	9 g

Using hot pepper sauce

Distilled from various varieties of chiles, hot pepper sauces are an excellent way to give a complex, fiery taste to savory foods. Just a few drops of sauce can produce an explosion of flavor, without adding a trace of calories or fat. Most hot sauces are relatively high in sodium, but are used in such limited quantities that they do not significantly raise the sodium level of the finished dish.

The best way to find one you like is to read labels and try brands that intrigue you because of the heat level they promise, the types of chiles that are used, or other flavorings that might be added.

Use hot pepper sauce with legume dishes, as here, or with all kinds of other savory preparations, from vegetables to grains, pastas to salads, soups to stews. Adding the sauce early in the cooking process tends to mute its flavor a bit, as some of the volatile chile flavors will evaporate. Add it just before serving to produce a more fiery effect.

Black-eyed peas and brown rice

This grain-and-legume mixture is a true Southern-style comfort food akin to Hoppin' John. Buy frozen, cooked black-eyed peas, or start with the dried legume and cook up a batch yourself (see page 160), freezing any extra for future meals.

SERVES: 6 | **PREPARATION:** 20 minutes | **COOKING:** 25 minutes

4 cups (28 oz/875 g) cooked, cold long-grain brown rice (see page 107)

1¼ cups (10 fl oz/310 ml) water

1 onion, chopped

2 celery stalks, chopped

2 garlic cloves, minced

¼ teaspoon ground pepper

3 cups (20 oz/625 g) frozen black-eyed peas

1 butternut squash, about 1 lb (500 g), peeled, seeded, and cut into cubes

1 red bell pepper (capsicum), stemmed, seeded, and finely chopped

½ teaspoon hot pepper sauce

♦ Put the rice in a large bowl and gently separate the grains and break apart any lumps.

♦ In a large frying pan, bring the water, onion, celery, garlic, and pepper to a boil, stirring frequently. Add the black-eyed peas and squash and return to a boil, stirring frequently. Reduce heat to low, cover, and simmer, stirring occasionally, until the peas and squash are tender and most of the water has evaporated, about 20 minutes.

♦ Add the rice, bell pepper, and pepper sauce and, stirring and tossing frequently, simmer until heated through, about 5 minutes.

♦ To serve, transfer to a bowl.

PER SERVING

Calories	323
Kilojoules	1,352
Protein	13 g
Carbohydrates	65 g
Total Fat	2 g
Saturated Fat	<1 g
Cholesterol	0 mg
Sodium	39 mg
Dietary Fiber	9 g

Summer vegetable and bean wrap

Call them vegetarian burritos, if you like. Eaten out of hand, these tidy little packages of quickly sautéed vegetables and beans are perfect to serve for a casual summer lunch. For even more Southwestern flair, pass bottled hot pepper sauce for guests to add to individual portions.

SERVES: 6 | **PREPARATION:** 30 minutes | **COOKING:** 20 minutes

2 teaspoons olive oil

1 garlic clove, minced

3 cups (15 oz/470 g) cooked pinto beans (see page 160) or canned pinto beans, rinsed and drained

2 red bell peppers (capsicums), stemmed, seeded, and cut into 3/4-inch (2-cm) squares

2 green bell peppers (capsicums), stemmed, seeded, and cut into 3/4-inch (2-cm) squares

4 zucchini (courgettes), halved lengthwise and thinly sliced

2 tomatoes, seeded and diced

4 green (spring) onions, thinly sliced, including green portions

1 tablespoon balsamic vinegar

1/2 cup (2/3 oz/20 g) chopped cilantro (fresh coriander)

12 whole wheat (wholemeal) tortillas, 10 inches (25 cm) in diameter

1/2 cup (4 oz/125 g) plain non-fat yogurt

◆ In a large nonstick frying pan over medium-high heat, heat the oil. Add the garlic and sauté until fragrant, 30 seconds to 1 minute. Add the beans and sauté for 2 minutes.

◆ Add the bell peppers and zucchini and continue to sauté until the vegetables are tender, 4–5 minutes.

◆ Add the tomatoes, green onions, and vinegar and continue to cook for 1 minute. Remove from heat and stir in the cilantro.

◆ Heat a dry large frying pan (not one with a nonstick surface) over medium heat. One at a time, heat the tortillas in the hot pan until softened, about 20 seconds per side.

◆ To serve, divide the tortillas among individual plates.

◆ Spread 2 teaspoons of the yogurt down the center of each tortilla. Divide the bean mixture among the tortillas. Fold in both sides and the bottom of each tortilla up over the filling, then roll to close.

cooking clinic

Seeding tomatoes

All tomatoes contain watery seed sacs that will dilute their flavor and that of the dishes to which they are added. For this reason, it is a good idea to seed tomatoes before using them in cooked dishes or tossed salads.

• *To seed a tomato, cut it in half crosswise to expose the seed sacs.*

• *If you are going to chop and cook the tomato, invert each half over a bowl or the sink and squeeze and shake it gently to force out the seeds and the watery pulp that surrounds them.*

• *If you will be slicing the tomatoes and want them to look neater, simply use the handle of a small teaspoon to gently scoop out the seed sacs.*

PER SERVING

Calories	392
Kilojoules	1,638
Protein	17 g
Carbohydrates	72 g
Total Fat	5 g
Saturated Fat	<1 g
Cholesterol	<1 mg
Sodium	497 mg
Dietary Fiber	11 g

Storing spices

Made from the dried seeds, flesh, barks, or roots of various plants, spices derive their flavor from volatile compounds that dissipate with prolonged exposure to light, heat, and air.

To get the most from your spices, buy them in small quantities—no more than you are likely to use within a few months. Buy whole spices, if possible, grinding only as much as you need in a spice mill or with a mortar and pestle just before use.

Store all spices, whether whole or already ground, in tightly covered containers at a cool room temperature in a dark place. If you notice any reduction in the aroma or taste of a spice you've had for a while, buy a new supply.

PER SERVING

Calories	409
Kilojoules	1,794
Protein	22 g
Carbohydrates	77 g
Total Fat	2 g
Saturated Fat	<1 g
Cholesterol	<1 mg
Sodium	60 mg
Dietary Fiber	8 g

Black bean chili over soft polenta

Two cuisines dynamically join forces in this combination of legumes and grains. Black bean chili is a favorite recipe of America's desert Southwest. Polenta, a signature Italian dish, is a natural accompaniment: Cornmeal came to Europe from the New World.

SERVES: 6 | **PREPARATION:** 30 minutes | **COOKING:** 1 hour

1 onion, chopped

1 green bell pepper (capsicum), stemmed, seeded, and chopped

2 celery stalks, chopped

3 garlic cloves, minced

2 tablespoons chili powder

1 tablespoon ground cumin

1 tablespoon paprika

2 tablespoons chopped fresh oregano or 2 teaspoons dried oregano

1/4 teaspoon cayenne pepper

3 tomatoes, coarsely chopped

6 cups (42 oz/1.35 kg) cooked black beans (see page 160) or canned black beans, rinsed and drained

1 1/2 cups (12 fl oz/375 ml) water

Polenta

6 cups (48 fl oz/1.5 l) water

1 cup (5 oz/155 g) cornmeal (maize flour)

6 tablespoons (3 oz/90 g) plain nonfat yogurt

6 cilantro (fresh coriander) sprigs

♦ Coat a large pot or dutch oven with nonstick cooking spray and place over medium-high heat. Add the onion, bell pepper, celery, garlic, chili powder, cumin, paprika, oregano, and cayenne. Sauté until the vegetables are softened but not browned, 7–10 minutes.

♦ Stir in the tomatoes, beans, and water and bring to a boil. Reduce heat to low and simmer, stirring occasionally, until the chili has thickened slightly and the flavors have blended, 30–40 minutes. If the chili is getting too thick, add 1/4 cup (2 fl oz/60 ml) additional water.

♦ To make the polenta, in a large saucepan, whisk together the water and 1/4 cup (1 1/4 oz/37 g) of the cornmeal until smooth. Bring to a boil. Gradually whisk in the remaining cornmeal. Reduce heat to low and simmer, stirring frequently, until the mixture thickens to the consistency of hot cereal, about 10 minutes.

♦ To serve, divide the polenta among individual plates. Top each with an equal amount of the chili, 1 tablespoon of the yogurt, and a cilantro sprig.

Cajun rotelle and red beans

For a hearty meal in minutes, mix pasta with the signature bean dish of Louisiana, complete with the kick of Cajun seasoning—a blend that usually includes paprika, cayenne, onion and garlic powders, white and black pepper, thyme, and oregano.

SERVES: 6　|　**PREPARATION:** 15 minutes　|　**COOKING:** 15 minutes

1 lb (500 g) dried rotelle pasta

1 onion, chopped

1 green bell pepper (capsicum), stemmed, seeded, and chopped

3 carrots, chopped

2 teaspoons Cajun seasoning

1 teaspoon ground cumin

1/4 teaspoon cayenne pepper

15 oz (470 g) canned red beans or kidney beans, drained and rinsed

2 tablespoons lemon juice

2 tablespoons chopped fresh oregano or 2 teaspoons dried oregano

◆ Fill a large pot three-quarters full of water and bring to a boil. Add the pasta and cook until al dente, about 10 minutes, or according to package directions.

◆ After the pasta has cooked for 3 minutes, remove 1 cup (8 fl oz/250 ml) of the cooking water. In a large frying pan over high heat, bring the reserved cooking water, onion, bell pepper, carrots, Cajun seasoning, cumin, and cayenne to a boil. Reduce heat to medium-high, cover, and cook, stirring occasionally, until the vegetables are barely tender, 3–5 minutes.

◆ Reduce heat to low and stir in the beans, lemon juice, and oregano.

◆ Drain the pasta thoroughly. Add the pasta to the beans. Stir and toss to combine.

◆ To serve, divide among individual plates.

cooking clinic

A guide to pasta shapes

Down through the centuries, Italian cooks have invented more than 400 pasta shapes. If you cannot find a particular shape called for in a recipe in this book, use one of similar size and shape listed here or one of the tiny pastas on page 136.

Bucatini. *Hollow, spaghettilike rods, also called perciatelli*

Farfalle. *"Butterflies," also known as bow ties*

Fettuccine. *"Ribbons" in Italian, describing the long, flat noodles*

Fusilli. *"Fuses," short, twisted strands*

Garganelli. *Small, ridged and folded tubes*

Gemelli. *"Twins," describing the short, intertwined strands*

Linguine. *"Small tongues," long, thin, flat strands*

Macaroni. *Curved tubes, short to medium-short in length*

Orecchiette. *Curved ear shapes*

Penne. *"Quill pens," tubes with angled ends resembling nibs*

Rotelle. *Medium twisted strands*

PER SERVING

Calories	368
Kilojoules	1,541
Protein	14 g
Carbohydrates	73 g
Total Fat	2 g
Saturated Fat	<1 g
Cholesterol	0 mg
Sodium	390 mg
Dietary Fiber	6 g

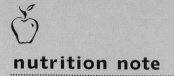
Fettuccine and summer tomatoes

Pasta doesn't get much easier or more colorful than spinach fettuccine topped with a mixture of fresh, sun-ripened tomatoes. If larger tomatoes are not at their peak, use cherry tomatoes instead. Here, a combination of red and yellow tomatoes yields an especially beautiful presentation.

SERVES: 6 | **PREPARATION:** 15 minutes | **COOKING:** 10 minutes

2 lb (1 kg) ripe tomatoes, stemmed and cut into 1/2-inch (12-mm) cubes

1 red (Spanish) onion, thinly sliced

1/3 cup (3 fl oz/80 ml) cider vinegar or white wine vinegar

1 tablespoon olive oil

2 tablespoons chopped fresh thyme or 2 teaspoons dried thyme

1/3 cup (1/3 oz/10 g) chopped flat-leaf (Italian) parsley

1/2 teaspoon ground pepper

1/4 teaspoon cayenne pepper

1 lb (500 g) dried spinach fettuccine

◆ In a large bowl, stir together the tomatoes, onion, vinegar, oil, thyme, parsley, pepper, and cayenne. Serve now, or cover and store at room temperature for up to 2 hours.

◆ Fill a large pot three-quarters full of water and bring to a boil. Add the pasta and cook until al dente, about 10 minutes, or according to package directions. Drain the pasta thoroughly.

◆ To serve, spread the pasta in a shallow serving bowl. Add the tomato mixture. Stir and toss to combine.

Winter squash and portobello penne

This earthy combination of pasta and vegetables topped with croutons is a complete meal in one bowl. The rustic-looking torn croutons will have a crunchier texture than neatly cut croutons. They take 40 minutes to bake but you can make them ahead.

SERVES: 6 | **PREPARATION:** 30 minutes | **COOKING:** 40 minutes croutons + 15 minutes pasta

Croutons

8 oz (250 g) unsliced whole wheat (wholemeal) bread

1 teaspoon dried oregano

1 teaspoon olive oil

12 oz (375 g) dried penne pasta

1 tablespoon olive oil

1/2 cup (4 fl oz/125 ml) water

3 onions, cut into 1/2-inch-thick (12-mm) slices and separated into rings

1 butternut squash, about 1 lb (500 g), peeled, seeded, and cut into 1/2-inch (12-mm) cubes

1/2 teaspoon ground pepper

12 oz (375 g) portobello mushrooms, sliced

2 tablespoons chopped fresh thyme or 2 teaspoons dried thyme

♦ To make the croutons, preheat an oven to 250°F (120°C). Trim the crusts from the bread and pull off pieces of bread roughly 1 inch (2.5 cm) square. In a large bowl, toss the bread with the oregano and olive oil. Spread in a single layer in a shallow baking pan and bake, without stirring, until dry and crisp, about 40 minutes. Cool completely. Serve now, or cover and store at room temperature for up to 2 weeks.

♦ Fill a large pot three-quarters full of water and bring to a boil. Add the pasta and cook until al dente, 10–12 minutes, or according to package directions.

♦ While the pasta cooks, in a large nonstick frying pan over medium-high heat, heat the olive oil and water. Add the onions, squash, and pepper and cook, stirring occasionally, until the onions have wilted and the squash is beginning to soften, about 10 minutes.

♦ Stir in the mushrooms, cover, and cook, stirring once, until the squash and mushrooms are tender, about 5 minutes.

♦ Remove 1 cup (8 fl oz/250 ml) of the cooking water, then drain the pasta thoroughly. Add the thyme and reserved cooking water to the vegetables.

♦ To serve, combine the pasta and vegetables in a large bowl. Top with the croutons.

nutrition note

Winter squashes

Hard-shelled winter squashes are one of the best sources of beta-carotene, one of many naturally occurring carotenoids in yellow and orange vegetables.

Like other carotenoids, beta-carotene's health benefits stem from its potent antioxidant effects. All winter squashes contain plentiful amounts of beta-carotene. Amounts range from the lowest in spaghetti and acorn squash to highest in deep-orange pumpkin.

PER SERVING

Calories	412
Kilojoules	1,724
Protein	14 g
Carbohydrates	80 g
Total Fat	6 g
Saturated Fat	<1 g
Cholesterol	0 mg
Sodium	192 mg
Dietary Fiber	8 g

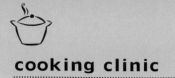

Preparing artichokes

In springtime, when artichokes are at their peak of season, use fresh artichoke hearts.

• *To prepare them, cut off the stem flush with the base.*

• *Beginning at the base, remove the leaves, snapping them downward and continuing round and round until you've revealed all the pale-green inner leaves.*

• *Cut off and discard the top cone. Then cut the artichoke in half lengthwise and use a sharp-edged spoon to scoop out the fibrous choke from both halves.*

• *Cut each half into wedges. Put them in a bowl of water mixed with lemon juice while you prepare the remaining artichokes.*

At other times of year, frozen artichoke hearts make a fine substitute. You can also find artichoke hearts in cans and jars, although they will have a softer texture and less pronounced flavor. Avoid artichoke hearts marinated in oil, which are higher in fat.

PER SERVING

Calories	431
Kilojoules	1,802
Protein	16 g
Carbohydrates	75 g
Total Fat	7 g
Saturated Fat	2 g
Cholesterol	5 mg
Sodium	148 mg
Dietary Fiber	16 g

Pasta with artichokes and carrots

Serve this quickly made pasta dish for an elegant dinner party. Some of the alcohol in the vermouth will evaporate, leaving behind the wonderfully fragrant flavor of this popular wine (see page 187). Be sure to select "dry" rather than "sweet" vermouth.

SERVES: 6 | **PREPARATION:** 15 minutes | **COOKING:** 10 minutes

1 lb (500 g) dried spinach fettuccine

1 tablespoon olive oil

16 oz (500 g) frozen artichoke hearts, cut lengthwise into thin strips

8 carrots, finely diced

1/4 teaspoon red pepper flakes

2 garlic cloves, minced

1/3 cup (3 fl oz/80 ml) dry vermouth

2 tablespoons lemon juice

2 tablespoons chopped fresh thyme or 2 teaspoons dried thyme

1/2 cup (21/2 oz/75 g) crumbled soft goat cheese

◆ Fill a large pot three-quarters full of water and bring to a boil. Add the pasta and cook until al dente, about 10 minutes, or according to package directions.

◆ While the pasta cooks, in a large nonstick frying pan over medium-high heat, heat the olive oil. Add the artichoke hearts, carrots, and pepper flakes and sauté until the carrots are tender, 5–7 minutes. Stir in the garlic and cook until fragrant, about 30 seconds longer. Add the vermouth, lemon juice, and thyme. Cook, stirring, 30 seconds longer.

◆ Remove 1/4 cup (2 fl oz/60 ml) of the cooking water, then drain the pasta thoroughly. Add the reserved cooking water and pasta to the vegetables. Stir and toss to combine.

◆ To serve, divide among individual plates. Top each with an equal amount of the goat cheese.

Shiitake and chicken tetrazzini

Replacing the cream that traditionally enriches this popular baked pasta dish is a mixture of evaporated milk and chicken broth, thickened with cornstarch to make a nonfat sauce that tastes exceptionally creamy. If you can't find shiitake mushrooms, substitute any other fresh variety.

SERVES: 6 | **PREPARATION:** 20 minutes | **COOKING:** 55 minutes

12 oz (375 g) dried spaghetti

3 tablespoons cornstarch (cornflour)

1½ cups (12 fl oz/375 ml) nonfat evaporated milk

2 cups (16 fl oz/500 ml) canned nonfat reduced-sodium chicken broth

½ teaspoon ground pepper

8 oz (250 g) shiitake mushrooms, thinly sliced

1 carrot, grated

⅓ cup (3 fl oz/90 ml) dry sherry

⅛ teaspoon ground nutmeg

Several drops hot pepper sauce

3 cups (1 lb/500 g) cooked, diced chicken breast meat

¼ cup (½ oz/15 g) fresh whole wheat (wholemeal) bread crumbs (see page 79)

3 tablespoons grated Parmesan cheese

◆ Fill a large pot three-quarters full of water and bring to a boil. Add the pasta and cook until al dente, about 10 minutes, or according to package directions.

◆ While the pasta cooks, preheat an oven to 375°F (190°C). Coat a 3-qt (3-l) baking dish with nonstick cooking spray.

◆ In a large saucepan over medium-high heat, whisk the cornstarch and evaporated milk until blended. Add the chicken broth and pepper. Bring to a boil, whisking frequently, then reduce heat to low. Simmer, whisking frequently, until the sauce has thickened slightly, about 5 minutes.

◆ Stir in the mushrooms and carrot, partially cover the pan, and simmer until the vegetables are tender, about 5 minutes. Stir in the sherry, nutmeg, pepper sauce, and chicken.

◆ Drain the pasta and put it in the prepared baking dish. Add the sauce and toss to combine. Sprinkle with the bread crumbs and cheese. Bake until the topping is lightly browned and the sauce is bubbling, 25–30 minutes.

◆ Cool 5 minutes before serving.

---

cooking clinic

Cooking chicken

Recipes that call for cooked chicken are a wonderful way for you to use leftover roasted, grilled, or broiled chicken.

• *If cooked chicken meat is not available, 1 pound (500 grams) of raw skinless, boneless chicken breast will give you 3 cups (1 lb/500 g) of shredded or chopped cooked meat.*

• *The easiest way to cook the chicken is by poaching: Into a saucepan, put enough water to cover the chicken completely. Bring to a boil, reduce heat to low, add the chicken, cover, and poach until cooked through, 10–15 minutes.*

• *If you don't plan to use the chicken immediately, refrigerate it in a tightly covered container in its cooking liquid.*

PER SERVING

Calories	455
Kilojoules	1,904
Protein	39 g
Carbohydrates	58 g
Total Fat	5 g
Saturated Fat	1 g
Cholesterol	69 mg
Sodium	388 mg
Dietary Fiber	2 g

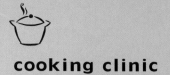

Cooking wild rice

Not a true rice at all, but the unpolished kernels of a wild grass native to Minnesota, wild rice is cooked differently than true rices (see page 107). Instead, wild rice requires boiling in a larger quantity of water.

• Fill a saucepan with enough water to cover the wild rice very generously. Bring the water to a boil and add the rice.

• Boil, uncovered, until the grains are tender, about 1 hour. Check toward the end of cooking to make sure the rice hasn't gone dry and begun to scorch, adding a little more boiling water if necessary.

• Pour through a fine-meshed strainer to drain before serving.

PER SERVING

Calories	345
Kilojoules	1,442
Protein	31 g
Carbohydrates	40 g
Total Fat	7 g
Saturated Fat	1 g
Cholesterol	64 mg
Sodium	221 mg
Dietary Fiber	1 g

Wild rice and chicken salad

Introducing fruit juice into a salad dressing adds intriguing flavor and texture without fat. Try substituting other juices or nectars for the pineapple juice called for here. Orange juice also marries well with the tastes of both the chicken breast and the wild rice.

SERVES: 6 | **PREPARATION:** 20 minutes

1/4 cup (2 fl oz/60 ml) pineapple juice

1 1/2 tablespoons white wine vinegar

1 tablespoon Dijon mustard

3 garlic cloves, crushed with a garlic press

1/2 teaspoon ground pepper

1 1/2 tablespoons olive oil

6 cups (32 oz/1 kg) cooked, cold wild rice

3 cups (1 lb/500 g) cooked, shredded chicken breast meat (see page 179)

1 red bell pepper (capsicum), stemmed, seeded, and cut into 1/2-inch (12-mm) squares

6 green (spring) onions, thinly sliced, including green portions

1/2 cup (1/3 oz/10 g) chopped fresh basil

1 1/2 tablespoons capers, drained

3 cups (4 1/2 oz/140 g) chopped romaine lettuce

♦ In a large bowl, whisk together the pineapple juice, vinegar, mustard, garlic, and pepper. Add the olive oil and whisk until well blended.

♦ Add the wild rice, chicken, bell pepper, green onions, basil, and capers. Stir and toss to coat well with the dressing. Add the lettuce and toss to mix well.

♦ To serve, divide among individual plates.

Chicken and vegetable casserole

Think of this as a New Mexican–style variation on traditional chicken pot pie. Black beans add dietary fiber to the filling, and chili powder contributes a hint of spice. In place of the usual pastry crust is a cornmeal biscuit topping spiked with mild green chiles.

SERVES: 6 | **PREPARATION:** 20 minutes | **COOKING:** 30 minutes

2 cups (12 oz/375 g) cooked, diced chicken breast meat (see page 179)

2 cups (12 oz/375 g) fresh cooked corn kernels or frozen corn kernels, thawed

2 cups (14 oz/440 g) cooked black beans (see page 160) or canned black beans, rinsed and drained

1 tablespoon chili powder

2 garlic cloves, minced

1/2 cup (4 fl oz/125 ml) tomato juice

1/2 cup (4 fl oz/125 ml) dry red or white wine

1/2 teaspoon ground pepper

1 tablespoon chopped fresh oregano or 1 teaspoon dried oregano

1 cup (5 oz/155 g) cornmeal (maize flour)

1/2 cup (2 1/2 oz/75 g) whole wheat (wholemeal) flour

2 teaspoons baking powder

1 1/2 teaspoons nonfat milk

1 egg plus 1 egg white

1/2 cup (4 oz/125 g) canned diced mild green chiles, drained

1/4 cup (1 oz/30 g) grated reduced-fat cheddar cheese

♦ Preheat an oven to 425°F (220°C). Coat a 3-qt (3-l) baking dish with nonstick cooking spray.

♦ In a large bowl, toss together the chicken, corn, beans, chili powder, garlic, juice, wine, pepper, and oregano. Spread in the prepared pan.

♦ Into a small bowl, sift together the cornmeal, flour, and baking powder.

♦ In a large bowl, whisk together the milk and egg and egg white until smooth. Stir in the chiles and cheese. Add the combined dry ingredients and stir briefly to combine. Do not worry if there are some lumps.

♦ Drop the cornmeal mixture by heaping tablespoons over the chicken mixture. Bake until the topping is browned and puffy, about 30 minutes.

♦ To serve, divide among individual soup plates.

PER SERVING

Calories	369
Kilojoules	1,543
Protein	30 g
Carbohydrates	53 g
Total Fat	5 g
Saturated Fat	2 g
Cholesterol	82 mg
Sodium	470 mg
Dietary Fiber	6 g

Oranges

Whether eaten whole or enjoyed as juice, an orange provides a day's supply of vitamin C. One orange is the equivalent of about 1/2 cup (4 fl oz/125 ml) juice. Oranges and orange juice are also a great way to get meaningful amounts of folic acid (folate).

Chickpea and citrus chicken salad

Canned chickpeas and prewashed and bagged salad greens allow you to put together this zesty chicken salad in just minutes. If you have no cooked chicken, consider a precooked rotisserie chicken from the market. Serve this salad as the centerpiece of a warm-weather meal.

SERVES: 6 | **PREPARATION:** 20 minutes

1/2 cup (4 fl oz/125 ml) orange juice

2 tablespoons plain nonfat yogurt

2 tablespoons lemon juice

2 garlic cloves, crushed with a garlic press

1 tablespoon Dijon mustard

1/2 teaspoon ground pepper

1 tablespoon olive oil

3 cups (1 lb/500 g) cooked, diced chicken breast meat (see page 179)

3 cups (18 oz/560 g) canned chickpeas (garbanzo beans), rinsed and drained

1 cucumber, peeled and cut into 1/2-inch-thick (12-mm) slices

1 small red (Spanish) onion, chopped

1/2 cup (3 oz/90 g) raisins

6 cups (4 oz/125 g) mixed salad greens

3/4 cup (1 oz/30 g) chopped fresh mint

♦ In a large bowl, whisk together the orange juice, yogurt, lemon juice, garlic, mustard, and pepper. Whisk in the olive oil until well blended. Add the chicken, beans, cucumber, onion, and raisins, stirring and tossing to coat well.

♦ To serve, divide the salad greens among individual plates. Top each with an equal amount of the chicken mixture. Sprinkle with the mint.

PER SERVING

Calories	397
Kilojoules	1,660
Protein	34 g
Carbohydrates	44 g
Total Fat	9 g
Saturated Fat	1 g
Cholesterol	64 mg
Sodium	412 mg
Dietary Fiber	9 g

Provençal chicken and fennel

The braised combination of chicken breasts, fennel, tomatoes, and garlic, accented by a fragrant hint of grated orange zest, brings to mind a casual supper you might enjoy in the south of France. Serve with the perfect complement: Golden Mashed Potatoes and Arugula (recipe on page 112).

SERVES: 6 | **PREPARATION:** 25 minutes | **COOKING:** 30 minutes

6 small fennel bulbs, 3 lb (1.5 kg) total, trimmed

2 tomatoes, diced or 14 1/2 oz (455 g) canned diced tomatoes, drained

1/4 cup (2 fl oz/60 ml) dry white wine

1 tablespoon grated orange zest

3 garlic cloves, minced

2 teaspoons balsamic vinegar

1/8 teaspoon red pepper flakes

6 skinless, bone-in chicken breast halves, 5 oz (155 g) each, trimmed of visible fat

2 tablespoons chopped fresh flat-leaf (Italian) parsley

♦ Cut each fennel bulb in half lengthwise through the base. Cut each half into 4 wedges.

♦ In a large nonstick frying pan, combine the tomatoes, wine, orange zest, garlic, vinegar, and pepper flakes. Cook over medium heat, stirring occasionally, until the mixture comes to a boil. Reduce heat to medium-low.

♦ Arrange the chicken and fennel over the tomato mixture, spooning a bit of the sauce over them. Cover and cook until the chicken is opaque throughout and the fennel is tender, about 25 minutes. Using a slotted spoon, transfer the chicken and vegetables to a warmed platter.

♦ Increase heat to high and cook, stirring occasionally, until the sauce has thickened slightly, about 5 minutes. Spoon the sauce over the chicken and vegetables and sprinkle with the parsley.

♦ To serve, divide among individual plates.

cooking clinic

Cooking with alcohol

Because alcohol boils at a lower temperature than water, it is commonly thought that much of it is eliminated when wine, beer, or spirits are cooked. However, not all the alcohol is removed. The total amount of alcohol remaining depends on the preparation method and the length of cooking.

For ideas to substitute alcohol in recipes, see page 207.

This chart, based on recent research conducted by the U.S. Department of Agriculture, shows the percentage of alcohol remaining after cooking.

PREPARATION METHOD	ALCOHOL REMAINING
Alcohol added to boiling liquid, removed from heat	85%
Flamed	75%
Stirred in and baked or simmered for:	
15 minutes	40%
30 minutes	35%
1 hour	25%
1 1/2 hours	20%
2 hours	10%
2 1/2 hours	5%

PER SERVING

Calories	163
Kilojoules	683
Protein	28 g
Carbohydrates	8 g
Total Fat	2 g
Saturated Fat	<1 g
Cholesterol	63 mg
Sodium	258 mg
Dietary Fiber	2 g

Honey chicken on Apricot wild rice

Sweet, spicy, and savory flavors combine the influences of both Asian and North African kitchens. Wheat germ adds a wonderfully nutlike texture to the chicken's coating while contributing less fat than would an equivalent quantity of nuts.

SERVES: 6 | **PREPARATION:** 10 minutes | **COOKING:** 40 minutes

3 tablespoons wheat germ

2 tablespoons honey

1 tablespoon Dijon mustard

1 tablespoon canned apricot nectar or apricot jam

3/4 teaspoon reduced-sodium soy sauce

6 skinless, bone-in chicken breast halves, 5 oz (155 g) each, trimmed of visible fat

Apricot Wild Rice (recipe follows)

♦ Preheat an oven to 375°F (190°C).

♦ In a small bowl, mix together the wheat germ, honey, mustard, apricot nectar or jam, and soy sauce until well blended.

♦ Arrange the chicken pieces, bone side down, on a baking sheet. Spread the wheat germ mixture evenly over the chicken breasts. Bake until the chicken is opaque throughout and the wheat germ mixture has formed a crust, 35–40 minutes.

♦ To serve, divide the rice among individual plates. Top each with a chicken breast half.

Apricot wild rice

MAKES: 6 cups (2 lb/1 kg) | **PREPARATION:** 20 minutes | **COOKING:** 1 hour

1 oz (30 g) dried shiitake mushrooms, stemmed

1 1/2 cups (12 fl oz/375 ml) warm water

2 cups (12 oz/375 g) wild rice, rinsed in a fine-mesh sieve under cold running water

1/2 cup (3 oz/90 g) coarsely chopped dried apricots

2 shallots, minced

♦ In a small bowl, soak the mushrooms in the warm water until barely softened, about 20 minutes. Remove the mushrooms, reserving the liquid. Coarsely chop the mushrooms. Strain the mushroom-soaking liquid through a fine-mesh sieve into a measuring cup. Add enough water to equal 5 cups (40 fl oz/1.25 l) liquid. Pour the liquid into a large saucepan and bring to a boil. Add the wild rice, mushrooms, apricots, and shallots. Return to a boil, cover, and reduce heat to low. Cook until the rice is tender and all the liquid has been absorbed, 45 minutes to 1 hour.

Pineapple-glazed chicken thighs

Although flavorful chicken thighs contain about twice the fat found in white meat, the amount is relatively low and acceptable. The tropical fruit flavor of this quickly cooked dish pairs excellently with Saffron Rice and Golden Raisin Pilaf (recipe on page 111).

SERVES: 6 | **PREPARATION:** 10 minutes | **COOKING:** 18 minutes

6 skinless, bone-in chicken thighs, 5 oz (155 g) each, trimmed of visible fat

3-inch (7.5-cm) piece fresh ginger, cut into 1/4-inch-thick (6-mm) slices

2/3 cup (5 fl oz/160 ml) pineapple juice

2 tablespoons reduced-sodium soy sauce

1 tablespoon sesame seeds

1 cup (6 oz/185 g) pineapple chunks

3 green (spring) onions, thinly sliced, including green portions

♦ Coat a large nonstick frying pan with nonstick cooking spray and place over medium heat. Add the chicken and ginger and cook, turning the chicken every few minutes, until the chicken is well browned on both sides, about 10 minutes.

♦ In a small bowl, stir together the pineapple juice and soy sauce. Pour into the frying pan and bring to a boil. Cover and cook for 3 minutes. Uncover and add the sesame seeds and pineapple chunks. Continue cooking, turning the chicken occasionally, until it is opaque throughout and the liquid remaining in the pan has reduced to a glaze, about 5 minutes.

♦ To serve, arrange the chicken, ginger, and pineapple on a large platter. Spoon an equal amount of glaze over each piece of chicken. Garnish with the green onions.

cooking clinic

Preparing pineapple

Always buy fully ripened pineapples. Testing for ripeness and sweetness is easy: Just sniff the fruit, which should have a strong, fresh, sweet aroma. As a further test, tug on one of the central leaves rising from the top of the fruit: It should pull out easily if the pineapple is fully ripe.

• *To prepare a whole pineapple, first use a large, sharp knife to cut off its crown and stem ends.*

• *Stand the fruit upright on one of its cut ends on a work surface. With the knife, cut off the peel in long strips from top to bottom.*

• *Examine the fruit for any tough, fibrous brown "eyes" remaining from the peel and cut them out with the tip of the knife.*

• *Just as you removed the peel, cut the fruit away from the approximately 1-inch-thick (2.5-cm) woody core that runs through its center.*

PER SERVING

Calories	172
Kilojoules	720
Protein	21 g
Carbohydrates	10 g
Total Fat	5 g
Saturated Fat	1 g
Cholesterol	86 mg
Sodium	291 mg
Dietary Fiber	1 g

Using a thermometer

To test for the doneness of any large cut of meat or poultry, or of a meat or poultry loaf such as this recipe, use an instant-read thermometer. Available in any well-stocked cookware store, this thin-stemmed instrument almost immediately registers the internal temperature of the item being cooked.

Begin testing at the earliest possible time given in the recipe. Insert the thermometer so that its tip reaches the center of the thickest part of the item being cooked. (Make sure it does not touch any bones in large roasts or whole poultry.) Wait about 20 seconds, then check the readout. Check every 5 minutes until the desired temperature is reached.

Baked vegetable-and-turkey loaf

Supplementing ground turkey with generous quantities of vegetables makes for a juicy and flavorful lower fat meat loaf. Partner the loaf with Baked Breaded Tomatoes shown here (recipe on page 79). Use any leftovers to make great sandwiches.

SERVES: 6 | **PREPARATION:** 15 minutes | **COOKING:** 45 minutes

1 lb (500 g) white mushrooms, finely chopped

5 carrots, grated

1 large zucchini (courgette), grated

1 small onion, finely chopped

1/2 lb (250 g) lean ground turkey

1 1/4 cups (4 oz/125 g) old-fashioned rolled oats

1 egg and 1 egg white

2 tablespoons chopped fresh flat-leaf (Italian) parsley

2 tablespoons Fresh Tomato Salsa (see page 99)

3 garlic cloves, minced

2 teaspoons Worcestershire sauce

2 teaspoons curry powder

♦ Preheat an oven to 375°F (190°C). Coat a baking sheet with nonstick cooking spray.

♦ In a large bowl, combine the mushrooms, carrots, zucchini, onion, turkey, oats, egg and egg white, parsley, salsa, garlic, Worcestershire, and curry. Mix thoroughly.

♦ Gently pat the mixture into a loaf-shaped mound about 9 inches (23 cm) long and place on the prepared baking sheet.

♦ Bake until the loaf is nicely browned on the outside and an instant-read thermometer inserted into the center registers 180°F (82°C), about 45 minutes.

♦ To serve, cut into slices.

PER SERVING

Calories	196
Kilojoules	820
Protein	14 g
Carbohydrates	24 g
Total Fat	6 g
Saturated Fat	1 g
Cholesterol	63 mg
Sodium	93 mg
Dietary Fiber	5 g

Sherried turkey on biscuits

Both elegant and homey, this turkey and vegetable dish has a nonfat creamy sauce that is perfect for serving with freshly baked biscuits. All you need to add for a perfectly balanced meal is a seasonal green vegetable such as the green beans shown here.

SERVES: 6 | **PREPARATION:** 25 minutes | **COOKING:** 25 minutes

Whole Wheat Biscuits dough (recipe on page 228)

1 cup (8 fl oz/250 ml) nonfat evaporated milk

3 tablespoons cornstarch (cornflour)

1 tablespoon canola oil

12 oz (375 g) white mushrooms, thinly sliced

1 red bell pepper (capsicum), seeded and finely chopped

1 carrot, peeled and thinly sliced crosswise

1 tablespoon all-purpose (plain) flour

1 cup (8 fl oz/250 ml) canned nonfat reduced-sodium chicken broth

1/2 cup (4 fl oz/125 ml) water

1/4 cup (2 fl oz/60 ml) dry sherry

2 tablespoons chopped fresh flat-leaf (Italian) parsley

2 cups (12 oz/375 g) cooked, diced, skinless turkey breast meat

◆ Preheat an oven to 425°F (220°C). Cover a baking sheet with aluminum foil.

◆ On a floured surface with floured hands, shape the biscuit dough into an 8-inch (20-cm) square, 1/4 inch (6 mm) thick. Using a sharp knife, cut the dough into 12 rectangular biscuits. Place them, barely touching, on the baking sheet. Bake the biscuits until lightly browned and puffy, 12–15 minutes.

◆ In a small bowl, whisk the evaporated milk and cornstarch until smooth.

◆ In a large saucepan over medium heat, heat the oil. When hot, add the mushrooms, bell pepper, and carrot and sauté until the vegetables are tender, about 5 minutes. Sprinkle with the flour and cook, stirring constantly, for 1 minute.

◆ Briefly whisk the milk and cornstarch again, then add to the saucepan, stirring until blended. Add the chicken broth and water and bring to a boil, stirring frequently. Add the sherry, parsley, and turkey and stir until the turkey is heated through, 2–3 minutes.

◆ To serve, split the biscuits and divide among individual plates. Spoon an equal amount of the turkey on each biscuit bottom. Cover with a biscuit top.

cooking clinic

Cooking turkey breast

Although the recipe at left is an ideal way to use up any turkey left over from a whole roast, you can also easily cook turkey expressly for it.

Look for turkey breast cutlets, slices of raw turkey breast 1/4–1/2 inch (6–12 mm) thick, cut from the breast. Although more expensive by weight than buying a whole turkey breast, they allow you the flexibility of buying and cooking only as much turkey as you need, with no waste.

Cook the breast cutlets simply by simmering them in a little water or nonfat reduced-sodium chicken broth. Bring the liquid to a boil, reduce heat to a simmer, and add the turkey cutlets. Cook over low heat until the turkey is tender and opaque throughout, about 10 minutes. If you won't be using them right away, refrigerate the cutlets in their cooking liquid to keep them moist.

PER SERVING

Calories	436
Kilojoules	1,825
Protein	30 g
Carbohydrates	59 g
Total Fat	8 g
Saturated Fat	3 g
Cholesterol	64 mg
Sodium	461 mg
Dietary Fiber	5 g

PER SERVING

Calories	131
Kilojoules	550
Protein	17 g
Carbohydrates	11 g
Total Fat	1 g
Saturated Fat	<1 g
Cholesterol	35 mg
Sodium	422 mg
Dietary Fiber	3 g

Swiss chard and turkey au gratin

Using packaged little onions will streamline the preparation of this Hungarian-influenced combination of greens and poultry without compromising its quality in any way. Serve with the Herbed Whole Wheat Popovers shown here (recipe on page 243).

SERVES: 6 | PREPARATION: 25 minutes | COOKING: 45 minutes

2 lb (1 kg) green or red Swiss chard, stemmed and cut crosswise into 1/2-inch (12-mm) strips

3 garlic cloves, minced

2 cups (16 fl oz/500 ml) water

1 cup (5 oz/155 g) frozen petite whole onions, thawed

3 skinless turkey breast cutlets, 4 oz (125 g) each, halved crosswise

1/2 teaspoon ground pepper

1/2 cup (4 fl oz/125 ml) dry white wine

2 teaspoons grated lemon zest

1 cup (8 fl oz/250 ml) canned nonfat reduced-sodium chicken broth

2 teaspoons paprika

2 tablespoons cornstarch (cornflour)

◆ Preheat an oven to 400°F (200°C). Coat a shallow 2-qt (2-l) baking dish with nonstick cooking spray.

◆ In a large pot or a dutch oven, combine the chard with the garlic and 1 cup (8 fl oz/250 ml) of the water. Cover and cook over medium-high heat, stirring once or twice, until the chard is wilted and barely tender, 10–15 minutes. Spread the chard mixture evenly in the prepared baking dish. Add the onions.

◆ Coat a large nonstick frying pan with nonstick cooking spray. Add the turkey cutlets in a single layer and sprinkle with the pepper. Cook, turning once, until the turkey is lightly browned on the outside but still pink in the center, about 3 minutes. Using a slotted spoon, remove the turkey and arrange on top of the chard.

◆ In the turkey pan, bring the wine and lemon zest to a boil. Boil, scraping any browned bits from the bottom of the pan, for 3 minutes. Add the chicken broth, 3/4 cup (6 fl oz/190 ml) of the remaining water, and 1 1/2 teaspoons of the paprika and return to a boil.

◆ In a small bowl, whisk the cornstarch with the remaining 1/4 cup (2 fl oz/60 ml) water until smooth. Add to the boiling broth, whisking constantly, until thickened, about 1 minute. Pour the cornstarch mixture over the turkey and chard.

◆ Bake until the turkey is fully cooked and the sauce is bubbling, about 20 minutes. Dust with the remaining paprika. Serve from the baking dish.

Lime scallops and orzo

The fresh, bright flavors of the Greek isles come through in this casual entree for a summer's day. If you can't find orzo, look for other tiny pasta shapes (see page 136). Take care not to overcook the scallops because their texture will change from tender to rubbery.

SERVES: 6 | **PREPARATION:** 10 minutes | **COOKING:** 15 minutes

1 lb (500 g) orzo pasta

4 fresh dill sprigs plus 1/3 cup (1/2 oz/15 g) chopped fresh dill

1 tablespoon olive oil

1 carrot, grated

1 lb (500 g) bay scallops or sea scallops cut into 1/2-inch (12-mm) chunks

1/2 teaspoon ground pepper

1/4 cup (2 fl oz/60 ml) lime juice

1 tablespoon finely grated lime zest

2 garlic cloves, minced

◆ Fill a large pot three-quarters full of water and bring to a boil. Add the orzo and dill sprigs and cook until the orzo is al dente, about 10 minutes, or according to package directions. Remove 1 cup (8 fl oz/250 ml) of the cooking water. Drain the orzo and remove and discard the dill sprigs.

◆ Coat a wok with nonstick cooking spray. Add the oil and place over medium-high heat. When hot, add the carrot and stir-fry for 1 minute.

◆ Add the scallops, orzo, and reserved cooking water and cook, stirring frequently, until most of the liquid has evaporated and the scallops are opaque throughout, 4–5 minutes.

◆ Stir in the pepper, chopped dill, lime juice, lime zest, and garlic.

◆ To serve, divide among individual plates.

PER SERVING

Calories	343
Kilojoules	1,437
Protein	21 g
Carbohydrates	54 g
Total Fat	4 g
Saturated Fat	<1 g
Cholesterol	25 mg
Sodium	133 mg
Dietary Fiber	2 g

Tomatillos are sometimes mistakenly referred to as green tomatoes because, with their round forms and glossy green skins, they do resemble small, unripened specimens of the popular vegetable-fruit. They have a tart, refreshing flavor that goes well with the robust, spicy tastes of dishes from the Southwest and Mexico.

You'll find fresh tomatillos in some Latin American markets and well-stocked food stores. Usually, these are sold still encased in their loose brown papery husks, which are easily peeled off by hand before the tomatillos are cut up.

If fresh tomatillos are unavailable, look for canned varieties in the specialty-food sections of most markets.

PER SERVING

Calories	258
Kilojoules	1,078
Protein	22 g
Carbohydrates	33 g
Total Fat	5 g
Saturated Fat	2 g
Cholesterol	121 mg
Sodium	448 mg
Dietary Fiber	4 g

Shrimp and black bean enchiladas

You'll see dishes such as this on the menus of some of the most innovative Southwestern restaurants around. You can also make the Black Bean Salsa on its own to use as a topping for grilled or broiled fish fillets or chicken breasts.

SERVES: 6 | **PREPARATION:** 30 minutes | **COOKING:** 25 minutes

Black Bean Salsa

10 oz (315 g) fresh tomatillos, husked, or 12 oz (375 g) canned tomatillos, drained

4 green (spring) onions, sliced, including green portions

3 garlic cloves, crushed with a garlic press

1/2 cup (4 oz/125 g) canned diced green chiles

1 jalapeño chile, halved, seeded, and minced

1/2 cup (3/4 oz/20 g) chopped cilantro (fresh coriander)

1/4 cup (1 1/2 oz/45 g) cooked black beans (see page 160) or canned black beans, rinsed and drained

1/4 cup (1 1/2 oz/45 g) fresh cooked corn kernels or frozen corn kernels, thawed

12 oz (375 g) cooked bay shrimp

1 tablespoon grated lemon zest

1/2 teaspoon ground pepper

12 corn tortillas, 8 inches (20 cm) in diameter

3/4 cup (3 oz/90 g) grated reduced-fat Monterey jack cheese

6 tablespoons (3 oz/90 g) plain nonfat yogurt

6 cilantro (fresh coriander) sprigs

♦ Preheat an oven to 400°F (200°C). Coat a large, shallow baking pan with nonstick cooking spray.

♦ To make the salsa, chop the tomatillos coarsely. In a blender or food processor, combine the tomatillos, onions, garlic, chiles, and cilantro. Process just until coarsely chopped. Stir in the beans and corn. Use now, or refrigerate in a tightly covered container for up to 3 days.

♦ In a large bowl, combine 2/3 cup (5 fl oz/160 ml) of the salsa, the shrimp, lemon zest, and pepper.

♦ Heat a dry large frying pan (not one with a nonstick surface) over medium heat. One at a time, heat the tortillas in the hot pan until softened, about 20 seconds per side.

♦ Lay the tortillas flat on a clean work surface. Spread an equal amount of the filling in the center of each tortilla, roll the tortilla around the filling, and place, seam-side down, in the prepared pan. Sprinkle with the cheese. Cover the pan loosely with aluminum foil.

♦ Bake for 15 minutes. Remove the foil and bake until the cheese is melted and the enchiladas are heated through, 7–10 minutes.

♦ To serve, place 2 enchiladas on individual plates. Top each pair with an equal amount of the remaining salsa, 1 tablespoon of the yogurt, and a cilantro sprig.

Sweet potato and shrimp gumbo

Part soup, part stew, and as widely varied as there are cooks in Louisiana, gumbo is the definitive classic of Cajun and Creole kitchens. The flavors hark back to the dish's roots in Africa. All include okra and often seafood, although versions also exist with chicken or sausage.

SERVES: 6 | **PREPARATION:** 25 minutes | **COOKING:** 30 minutes

3/4 cup (6 fl oz/180 ml) tomato juice

1 onion, chopped

1 green bell pepper (capsicum), stemmed, seeded, and chopped

1/2 lb (250 g) okra, stemmed and thinly sliced

2 celery stalks, chopped

2/3 cup (5 fl oz/160 ml) dry white wine

1/4 cup (2 fl oz/60 ml) distilled white vinegar

1 lb (500 g) sweet potatoes, peeled and cut into 1-inch (2.5-cm) cubes

3 cups (28 oz/875 g) canned crushed tomatoes or tomato purée

1 1/2 tablespoons chili powder

1/8 teaspoon cayenne pepper

24 fresh or thawed frozen shrimp (prawns), shelled and deveined

6 cups (32 oz/1 kg) cooked, hot white rice (see page 107)

◆ In a large frying pan over medium-high heat, heat the tomato juice. Add the onion, bell pepper, okra, and celery and sauté until wilted and softened slightly, 5–7 minutes.

◆ Add the wine and vinegar and bring to a boil. Stir in the sweet potatoes, tomatoes or purée, chili powder, and cayenne and cook until it returns to a boil. Reduce heat to low, cover, and simmer, stirring occasionally, until the sweet potatoes are tender, 15–18 minutes.

◆ Add the shrimp and stir to combine. Cover and cook until the shrimp are pink, about 5 minutes.

◆ To serve, divide the rice among individual bowls. Top each with an equal amount of the gumbo.

Cooking fish

The culinary rule of thumb, whether baking, broiling, grilling, or poaching, is to cook fish for 8–10 minutes per 1 inch (2.5 cm) of thickness measured at the thickest point.

Test for doneness at the earliest time given in the recipe to prevent fish from overcooking and losing its moist, tender texture. To test, use the tip of a small, sharp knife to make a slit in the fish. The flesh should flake easily and appear opaque at its center.

Lemon-pepper trout over quinoa

Trout has a delicacy of taste and texture that finds perfect highlights in the simple seasonings of lemon juice and black pepper used here. To ease the preparation, ask your fishmonger to butterfly and bone the fish and remove their heads for you at the market.

SERVES: 6 | **PREPARATION:** 15 minutes | **COOKING:** 25 minutes

1½ cups (9 oz/280 g) quinoa

1½ cups (12 fl oz/375 ml) canned vegetable broth

1½ cups (12 fl oz/375 ml) water

2 carrots, diced

1 onion, diced

3 boneless butterflied trout, 9 oz (280 g) each, halved lengthwise

2 tablespoons lemon juice

½ teaspoon ground pepper

2 tablespoons chopped fresh flat-leaf (Italian) parsley

6 lemon wedges

♦ Put the quinoa in a bowl and add cold water to cover. Stir gently with a fork for 1 minute. Drain through a fine-mesh sieve, then rinse under cold running water for 1 minute. Drain thoroughly, 4–5 minutes.

♦ In a large saucepan, bring the broth and water to a boil. Add the carrots and onion and cook, stirring occasionally, until it returns to a boil. Stir in the quinoa, cover, and reduce heat to low. Simmer until the quinoa is tender and the liquid is absorbed, about 15 minutes.

♦ Preheat a broiler (griller). Coat a broiler rack with nonstick cooking spray.

♦ Place the fish on the prepared rack, flesh side up. Drizzle each with 1 teaspoon lemon juice and season with the pepper.

♦ Position the broiler rack about 4 inches (10 cm) from the heat.

♦ Broil the fish until opaque throughout, about 5 minutes.

♦ To serve, mound the quinoa mixture on a platter. Top with the fish. Sprinkle with the parsley. Garnish with the lemon wedges.

Calories	380
Kilojoules	1,589
Protein	33 g
Carbohydrates	37 g
Total Fat	11 g
Saturated Fat	2 g
Cholesterol	74 mg
Sodium	354 mg
Dietary Fiber	7 g

Tuscan tuna and cannellini beans

Tuna and white beans, or Tonno e fagioli, is one of the favorite combinations of Tuscan kitchens, enjoyed for the way the creaminess of the legumes complements the firm-textured fish. Here, orange juice and zest add a wonderfully fruity flavor that highlights both featured ingredients.

SERVES: 6 | **PREPARATION:** 15 minutes | **COOKING:** 20 minutes

1/3 cup (3 fl oz/80 ml) orange juice

1 onion, chopped

2/3 cup (5 fl oz/160 ml) dry vermouth or dry white wine

1/4 cup (2 fl oz/60 ml) white wine vinegar

1 lb (500 g) fresh tuna steaks, cut into 1-inch (2.5-cm) cubes

4 cups (28 oz/875 g) cooked cannellini beans (see page 160) or canned cannellini beans, rinsed and drained

2 tomatoes, coarsely chopped

1/4 cup (1/3 oz/10 g) chopped fresh basil

1/2 teaspoon ground pepper

2 tablespoons grated orange zest

1 tablespoon chopped chives

◆ In a large nonstick frying pan over medium-high heat, heat the orange juice. Add the onion and sauté until wilted, about 5 minutes. Add the vermouth or wine and vinegar and continue to sauté for 2 minutes.

◆ Reduce heat to medium and stir in the fish, beans, tomatoes, basil, pepper, and half the orange zest. Cover and cook until the fish is opaque throughout, 7–9 minutes.

◆ To serve, divide among individual plates. Sprinkle with the chives and remaining orange zest.

cooking clinic

Substitutes for alcohol

Although some of the alcohol is eliminated in cooking (see page 187), to avoid using alcohol in cooking, consider these substitutes.

For 1 cup (8 fl oz/250 ml) of wine or spirits:

- *7/8 cup (7 fl oz/220 ml) chicken broth and 1/8 cup (1 fl oz/30 ml) lemon juice or vinegar.*

- *7/8 cup (7 fl oz/220 ml) fruit juice and 1/8 cup (1 fl oz/30 ml) lemon juice or vinegar.*

- *An equal amount of nonalcoholic wine.*

- *Water and flavored vinegar, such as raspberry or tarragon, to taste.*

- *Water and similarly flavored extracts (essences), to taste.*

PER SERVING

Calories	341
Kilojoules	1,426
Protein	30 g
Carbohydrates	38 g
Total Fat	5 g
Saturated Fat	1 g
Cholesterol	29 mg
Sodium	39 mg
Dietary Fiber	6 g

Using salsa

As the recipe on this page demonstrates, fresh salsas of the American Southwest, Mexico, and other Latin American lands offer a healthful way to add excitement to food with little extra fat or sodium.

Most salsas include some form of chile pepper for its mild-to-fiery heat. Fresh herbs add an aromatic bouquet and citrus juice an acidic bite. Still other ingredients can also be added, including tomatoes (see recipe on page 99), and even melon (page 215) or tropical fruit. Chopped onion, shallots, or garlic are also favorite additions. After you've tried a few, feel free to experiment with your own combinations.

Although fresh salsas are easy to make, most well-stocked food stores stock fresh salsas in their refrigerated food cases.

PER SERVING

Calories	216
Kilojoules	903
Protein	28 g
Carbohydrates	17 g
Total Fat	3 g
Saturated Fat	<1 g
Cholesterol	58 mg
Sodium	150 mg
Dietary Fiber	2 g

Cilantro salsa and sea bass

Braising sea bass fillets on a bed of well-seasoned carrots and potatoes keeps the fish incomparably moist while lending it delicious flavor. The topping of fresh herbs, chiles, and lime juice fills the air with tantalizing aromas when it is spooned onto each individual serving.

SERVES: 6 | **PREPARATION:** 25 minutes | **COOKING:** 30 minutes

Cilantro Salsa

1/4 teaspoon sugar

2 tablespoons lime juice

1/3 cup (1/2 oz/15 g) chopped cilantro (fresh coriander)

1/4 cup (2 oz/60 g) canned diced green chiles

1/8 teaspoon chile oil

3/4 cup (6 fl oz/180 ml) dry white wine

3/4 cup (6 fl oz/180 ml) water

1/2 teaspoon chili powder

1/8 teaspoon cayenne pepper

1 bay leaf

1 lb (500 g) red-skinned potatoes, cut into quarters

2 carrots, cut into 2-inch (5-cm) pieces

6 sea bass fillets, 5 oz (155 g) each

♦ To make the salsa, in a small bowl, mix the sugar and lime juice until the sugar dissolves. Stir in the cilantro, chiles, and chile oil.

♦ In a large nonstick frying pan, bring the wine, water, chili powder, cayenne, and bay leaf to a boil. Add the potatoes and carrots. Reduce heat to medium-high, cover, and cook until the vegetables are barely tender, about 20 minutes.

♦ Arrange the fish fillets on top of the vegetables and reduce heat to medium. Cover and cook until the fish is opaque throughout, about 10 minutes. Remove and discard the bay leaf.

♦ To serve, divide the fish and vegetables among individual soup plates. Top each with an equal amount of the salsa.

Baked cod on a polenta-pepper bed

Layering spinach, bell pepper-flavored polenta, and fresh fish fillets in a baking dish produces a quick one-dish meal full of color and flavor. In place of the cod, try substituting other firm-fleshed white fish such as sea bass or halibut.

SERVES: 6 | **PREPARATION:** 20 minutes | **COOKING:** 25 minutes

Polenta

4 cups (32 fl oz/1 l) water

1 cup (5 oz/155 g) cornmeal (maize flour)

1/2 cup (21/2 oz/75 g) chopped roasted (see page 99) red bell peppers (capsicums)

11/2 tablespoons chopped fresh thyme or flat-leaf (Italian) parsley

11/2 cups (101/2 oz/330 g) cooked chopped spinach or thawed and drained frozen spinach

2 tablespoons lemon juice

1 tablespoon olive oil

6 cod fillets, 4 oz (125 g) each

12 lemon wedges

◆ Preheat an oven to 400°F (200°C). Coat a 9 x 13-inch (23 x 33-cm) baking dish with nonstick cooking spray.

◆ To make the polenta, in a large, heavy saucepan, whisk together the water and 1/4 cup (11/4 oz/37 g) of the cornmeal. Bring to a boil. In a slow, steady stream, gradually whisk in the remaining cornmeal. Reduce heat to low and simmer, stirring frequently, until the mixture thickens to the consistency of hot cereal, about 10 minutes. Remove from heat and stir in the red peppers and thyme or parsley. Spread in the prepared baking dish.

◆ In a small bowl, toss together the spinach, lemon juice, and olive oil. Scatter the spinach over the polenta. Place the fish fillets in a single layer on top of the spinach, pressing them into the polenta slightly.

◆ Bake until the fish is opaque throughout, about 15 minutes.

◆ To serve, divide among individual plates. Pass the lemon wedges at the table.

Discovering cornmeal

A staple grain of the Italian kitchen, polenta is a cooked mush of cornmeal. You can serve it as a first course, complement, or as the base for other dishes such as the recipe at left.

The term polenta also refers to the yellow or white Italian cornmeal from which the mush is made. Make polenta from regular cornmeal or from the imported product, labeled "polenta," in well-stocked food stores. Be sure to get the long-cooking variety, avoiding quick-cooking products that lack the dish's signature rich flavor and robust consistency.

PER SERVING

Calories	221
Kilojoules	926
Protein	24 g
Carbohydrates	24 g
Total Fat	4 g
Saturated Fat	<1 g
Cholesterol	49 mg
Sodium	121 mg
Dietary Fiber	2 g

Red snapper on couscous with peas

Combining the taste of North Africa and the flavor of India, this entree is easy to make and delicious. Dusted with paprika and steamed on top of the tiny grains of semolina pasta, the red snapper turns out moist, tender, and very flavorful.

SERVES: 6 | **PREPARATION:** 10 minutes | **COOKING:** 20 minutes

1/4 cup (2 fl oz/60 ml) orange juice

1 small onion, chopped

1 1/2 cups (10 oz/315 g) frozen peas

1/4 teaspoon salt

1 teaspoon ground cumin

1 teaspoon curry powder

2 1/4 cups (18 fl oz/560 ml) water

1 1/2 cups (10 oz/315 g) couscous

8 oz (250 g) canned chickpeas (garbanzo beans), drained and rinsed

2 tablespoons lemon juice

6 red snapper fillets, 5 oz (155 g) each

1/2 teaspoon paprika

♦ In a large nonstick frying pan over medium-high heat, heat the orange juice. Add the onion and sauté until wilted, 3–5 minutes. Stir in the peas, salt, cumin, and curry powder and sauté for 1 minute.

♦ Add the water and bring to a boil. Stir in the couscous, chickpeas, and lemon juice. Reduce heat to low.

♦ Arrange a single layer of the fish fillets on top of the couscous and dust with the paprika. Cover and simmer until the fish is opaque throughout and the couscous has absorbed all the liquid, about 10 minutes.

♦ To serve, divide among individual plates.

PER SERVING

Calories	397
Kilojoules	1,662
Protein	39 g
Carbohydrates	50 g
Total Fat	3 g
Saturated Fat	<1 g
Cholesterol	52 mg
Sodium	288 mg
Dietary Fiber	5 g

Poached salmon with melon salsa

Oven-poaching seafood inside a foil envelope, a technique called en papillote *in French, seals in moisture and flavor and greets diners with a burst of fragrant steam when the packets are carefully opened. Borrowing a practice common in tropical kitchens, fresh fruit tops the fish.*

SERVES: 6 | **PREPARATION:** 40 minutes | **COOKING:** 15 minutes

2 green (spring) onions, thinly sliced, including green portions

1½ teaspoons chopped fresh mint

1 teaspoon grated fresh ginger

3 tablespoons grated lime zest

1½ lb (750 g) salmon fillets, skinned and cut into 6 pieces

Melon Salsa

1 honeydew melon, about 3 lb (1.5 kg), peeled, seeded, and cut into ½-inch (12-mm) cubes

1 yellow bell pepper (capsicum), seeded, stemmed, and cut into ½-inch (12-mm) squares

¼ cup (2 fl oz/60 ml) lime juice

½ red (Spanish) onion, chopped

1 jalapeño chile, minced

2 tablespoons chopped fresh mint

♦ Preheat an oven to 450°F (230°C).

♦ In a small bowl, toss together the onions, mint, ginger, and lime zest.

♦ Place 6 pieces of aluminum foil, each 10 inches (25 cm) square, onto a work surface. Place a piece of salmon in the center of each square. Top each with an equal amount of the onion mixture. Fold in the edges of the foil and crimp to seal. Place the packets in a single layer on a baking sheet and bake until opaque throughout, 12–15 minutes.

♦ Meanwhile, to make the salsa, in a medium bowl, toss together the melon, pepper, lime juice, onion, jalapeño, and mint.

♦ To serve, transfer the contents of each packet onto an individual plate. Top each with an equal amount of the salsa.

PER SERVING

Calories	261
Kilojoules	1,093
Protein	24 g
Carbohydrates	14 g
Total Fat	12 g
Saturated Fat	2 g
Cholesterol	67 mg
Sodium	83 mg
Dietary Fiber	2 g

To make sure you get the full impact of garlic's pungent flavor, buy it only in whole heads, separating the individual garlic cloves from the head as you need them. Do not buy any more garlic than you are likely to use within a few weeks, as the cloves can shrivel and lose their flavor under prolonged storage. Store the heads in a cool, dry pantry, away from heat and light.

• *To peel a garlic clove, put it on a work surface and cover it with the side of a large chef's knife.*

• *Press down firmly but carefully on the side of the knife, crushing the clove slightly. This will loosen the dry skin, which will slip off easily.*

• *Slice, chop, or mince the clove with a knife, or press it through the holes of a garlic press, as called for in the recipe.*

PER SERVING

Calories	354
Kilojoules	1,482
Protein	32 g
Carbohydrates	43 g
Total Fat	7 g
Saturated Fat	2 g
Cholesterol	51 mg
Sodium	61 mg
Dietary Fiber	7 g

Rosemary lamb and white beans

One lamb chop is a perfect little package of red meat served with well-seasoned white beans in a robust and satisfying entree. To round out the meal, serve a green vegetable such as the Tender Spring Peas and Asparagus shown here (recipe on page 83).

SERVES: 6 | **PREPARATION:** 10 minutes | **MARINATING:** 30 minutes | **COOKING:** 30 minutes

1½ teaspoons finely chopped fresh rosemary or ½ teaspoon dried rosemary

2 garlic cloves, crushed with a garlic press

½ teaspoon olive oil

6 loin lamb chops, 5 oz (155 g) each, trimmed of visible fat

Beans

4½ cups (2 lb/1 kg) cooked white beans (see page 160) or canned white beans, rinsed and drained

1½ cups (9 oz/280 g) diced fresh tomatoes or canned diced tomatoes, drained

1 small onion, finely chopped

½ cup (¾ oz/20 g) chopped fresh flat-leaf (Italian) parsley

1½ teaspoons chopped fresh rosemary or ½ teaspoon dried rosemary

3 garlic cloves, minced

¾ teaspoon ground pepper

6 small rosemary sprigs

♦ In a small bowl, combine the rosemary, garlic, and olive oil. Rub the mixture evenly into both sides of the lamb chops. Cover and marinate at room temperature for 30 minutes.

♦ For the beans, preheat an oven to 425°F (220°C). Coat a 2-qt (2-l) shallow baking dish with nonstick cooking spray.

♦ In a large bowl, combine the beans, tomatoes, onion, parsley, rosemary, garlic, and pepper.

♦ Spread the bean mixture into the prepared dish. Cover and bake until heated through, about 15 minutes.

♦ Meanwhile, preheat a broiler (griller). Arrange the lamb chops on a broiler pan and place the pan 4 inches (10 cm) from the heat. Broil, turning once, until lightly browned on both sides, 6–7 minutes total.

♦ Remove the dish from the oven and arrange the lamb chops on top of the beans, pressing down gently. Return to the oven and cook, uncovered, until the beans are lightly browned on top and the chops are fully cooked, about 10 minutes.

♦ To serve, divide the beans and lamb chops among individual plates. Garnish with the rosemary sprigs.

Pork and plum sauté on prune bulgur

Most pork is remarkably lean. Of course, lean meat requires moist cooking methods to prevent it from drying out, which is why this sauté is so good. The prunes, plums, apple, and raisins add moisture and enhance the pork's mild, slightly sweet flavor.

SERVES: 6 | **PREPARATION:** 15 minutes | **COOKING:** 35 minutes

1½ cups (9 oz/280 g) bulgur wheat

½ teaspoon ground pepper

2¾ cups (22 fl oz/680 ml) boiling water

1 onion, chopped

1 lb (500 g) pork tenderloin, trimmed of visible fat and cut into cubes

¾ cup (7 oz/220 g) Plum Chutney (recipe follows)

½ cup (4 fl oz/125 ml) cold water

½ cup (3 oz/90 g) finely diced pitted prunes

♦ In a large saucepan over medium heat, toast the bulgur and pepper, stirring constantly, until the bulgur has darkened slightly, 3–4 minutes. Carefully add the boiling water, reduce heat to low, cover, and simmer until the bulgur has absorbed the water, about 20 minutes.

♦ Coat a large nonstick frying pan with nonstick cooking spray and heat over medium-high heat. Add the onion and pork and sauté until lightly browned, about 5 minutes.

♦ Stir in the chutney and the cold water. Reduce heat to medium, cover, and cook, stirring and tossing twice, until the pork is fully cooked, 4–5 minutes.

♦ Stir the prunes into the bulgur.

♦ To serve, mound the bulgur on a large platter. Top with the pork.

PER SERVING

Calories	333
Kilojoules	1,395
Protein	22 g
Carbohydrates	57 g
Total Fat	4 g
Saturated Fat	<1 g
Cholesterol	49 mg
Sodium	47 mg
Dietary Fiber	10 g

Plum chutney

MAKES: 2¼ cups (21 oz/655 g) | **PREPARATION:** 15 minutes | **COOKING:** 35 minutes

1¼ lb (625 g) plums

1 large apple

⅓ cup (2 oz/60 g) golden raisins (sultanas)

2 tablespoons grated fresh ginger

⅓ cup (3 oz/90 g) sugar

½ cup (4 fl oz/125 ml) white vinegar

2 teaspoons curry powder

1 cinnamon stick, halved

♦ Peel, pit, and chop the plums. Peel, core, and dice the apple. In a saucepan, bring the plums, apple, raisins, ginger, sugar, vinegar, curry powder, and cinnamon stick to a boil, stirring frequently. Reduce heat to low and simmer, stirring occasionally, until the fruit is tender, 30–35 minutes. Remove and discard the cinnamon stick.

PER TABLESPOON

Calories	25
Kilojoules	107
Protein	<1 g
Carbohydrates	6 g
Total Fat	<1 g
Saturated Fat	0 g
Cholesterol	0 mg
Sodium	<1 mg
Dietary Fiber	<1 g

Tomato poached pork on Currant kasha

This dish offers all the pleasures of traditional sweet-and-sour pork with just a fraction of the fat, because the bite-sized chunks are simmered in their sauce instead of deep-fried. To add more fruit to your meal, present the pork, as shown here, on a bed of sliced apple, with the kasha on the side.

SERVES: 6 | **PREPARATION:** 15 minutes | **MARINATING:** 30 minutes | **COOKING:** 15 minutes

1½ cups (12 fl oz/375 ml) tomato juice

2 tablespoons balsamic vinegar

4 garlic cloves, minced

2 teaspoons reduced-sodium soy sauce

1 teaspoon honey

¼ teaspoon red pepper flakes

1½ lb (750 g) pork tenderloin, trimmed of visible fat and cut into 1-inch (2.5-cm) cubes

Currant Kasha (recipe follows)

♦ To make the marinade, in a large bowl, whisk together the tomato juice, vinegar, garlic, soy sauce, honey, and pepper flakes. Remove and reserve half of the marinade.

♦ Add the pork to the large bowl of marinade, stirring to coat. Cover and marinate at room temperature for 30 minutes.

♦ Using a slotted spoon, remove the meat, then discard the marinade.

♦ In a nonstick wok or large frying pan over high heat, bring the reserved marinade to a boil. Reduce heat to medium and boil for 2 minutes. Add the pork, cover, and cook for 5 minutes. Uncover and continue to cook until the pork is cooked through and the sauce has thickened, about 5 minutes.

♦ To serve, divide the kasha among individual plates. Top each with an equal amount of the pork and sauce.

Currant kasha

MAKES: 6 cups (48 oz/1.5 kg) | **PREPARATION:** 10 minutes | **COOKING:** 15 minutes

1½ cups (12 oz/375 g) kasha, medium granulation

3 cups (24 fl oz/750 ml) boiling water

¾ cup (5 oz/155 g) dried currants

⅛ teaspoon ground pepper

2 tablespoons chopped fresh flat-leaf (Italian) parsley

♦ Heat a dry large frying pan (not one with a nonstick surface) over medium-high heat. Toast the kasha, stirring, until dark brown and hot, 2–3 minutes. Reduce heat to low. Stir in the boiling water, currants, and pepper. Cover and cook until the kasha is just tender and the liquid is absorbed, 10–12 minutes. Stir in the parsley before serving.

Teriyaki vegetable and beef kabobs

While meat in moderation can be part of eating well, the nutritional analysis for each kabob on this page clearly indicates the increase in fat when you add meat to a recipe. The vegetable-only version of these Japanese-inspired kabobs replaces the beef with chunks of eggplant.

MAKES: 18 │ **PREPARATION:** 25 minutes │ **MARINATING:** 30 minutes │ **COOKING:** 10 minutes

Marinade

1/2 cup (4 fl oz/125 ml) reduced-sodium soy sauce

4 garlic cloves, crushed with a garlic press

2 teaspoons grated fresh ginger

2 teaspoons lime juice

2 teaspoons honey

1/4 teaspoon red pepper flakes

1/4 teaspoon sesame oil

1 lb (500 g) beef tenderloin, trimmed of visible fat and cut into 1-inch (2.5-cm) cubes

3 Japanese eggplants (aubergines), cut crosswise into 1/2-inch (12-mm) pieces

1 1/4 lb (625 g) white mushrooms

2 zucchini (courgettes), cut crosswise into 1/2-inch (12-mm) pieces

2 yellow squash, cut crosswise into 1/2-inch (12-mm) pieces

2 red bell peppers (capsicums), stemmed, seeded, and cut into 3/4-inch (2-cm) squares

2 red (Spanish) onions, cut into 1/2-inch-thick (12-mm) wedges

♦ To make the marinade, in a large bowl, whisk together the soy sauce, garlic, ginger, lime juice, honey, pepper flakes, and sesame oil. Transfer 3 tablespoons of the marinade to a medium bowl. Add the beef to the medium bowl, tossing to coat. Add the eggplants, mushrooms, zucchini, squash, peppers, and onions to the large bowl, tossing to coat.

♦ Cover and marinate both the meat and vegetables at room temperature for 30 minutes, tossing once or twice.

♦ Meanwhile, preheat a broiler (griller). Line the broiler pan with aluminum foil and coat with nonstick cooking spray. Soak 18 long wooden skewers in water to cover.

♦ Using a slotted spoon, remove the meat and vegetables from the bowls and pat dry with paper towels. Discard the meat marinade.

♦ For the 6 beef kabobs, divide the meat cubes equally among 6 skewers, threading it alternately with one third of the mushrooms, zucchini, squash, peppers, and onions.

♦ For the 12 vegetable kabobs, thread the eggplant pieces onto 12 skewers, alternating with the remaining mushrooms, zucchini, squash, peppers, and onions.

♦ Working in batches if necessary, place the kabobs 2 inches (5 cm) apart on the broiler pan. Position the pan 4 inches (10 cm) from the heat source. Broil, turning once or twice and brushing the kabobs with any remaining vegetable marinade, until the vegetables are tender and the beef is nicely browned, 8–10 minutes.

♦ To serve, divide among individual plates.

PER VEGETABLE KABOB

Calories	35
Kilojoules	147
Protein	2 g
Carbohydrates	7 g
Total Fat	<1 g
Saturated Fat	0 g
Cholesterol	0 mg
Sodium	181 mg
Dietary Fiber	1 g

PER BEEF KABOB

Calories	160
Kilojoules	670
Protein	18 g
Carbohydrates	8 g
Total Fat	6 g
Saturated Fat	2 g
Cholesterol	48 mg
Sodium	393 mg
Dietary Fiber	1 g

Trimming the fat

Saturated fat raises your blood cholesterol level more than anything else you eat. Red meat is a major source of saturated fat, but reducing fat doesn't mean bypassing the meat counter. To control saturated fat while still enjoying red meat:

• Choose lean cuts. The amount of fat in meat varies with the amount of marbling. To reduce fat, choose the leanest cuts with the least marbling such as round or loin cuts. Among grades, "select" meats are lowest in fat and calories. "Choice" contains more fat and calories than select and "prime" has the highest proportion of fat.

• Trim the fat. The real key to lean protein is paring visible fat. Trimming fat from a lean roast before cooking prevents fat from migrating into the meat. This further reduces fat without any loss of flavor.

PER SERVING

Calories	226
Kilojoules	946
Protein	20 g
Carbohydrates	18 g
Total Fat	8 g
Saturated Fat	3 g
Cholesterol	47 mg
Sodium	203 mg
Dietary Fiber	3 g

Balsamic beef and arugula salad

This salad demonstrates a key principle of eating well, with thin, flavorful strips of meat forming a garnish for a generous helping of salad greens. The greens, in fact, are the featured ingredient, even though you appear to be serving a beef dish.

SERVES: 6 | **PREPARATION:** 15 minutes | **COOKING:** 15 minutes

1 bunch arugula (rocket), about 4 oz (125 g), stemmed

4 cups (4 oz/125 g) mixed salad greens

1/3 cup (2 oz/60 g) minced shallots or finely chopped green (spring) onions, white portion only

6 oz (185 g) mushrooms, thinly sliced

1/2 teaspoon ground pepper

1 lb (500 g) beef tenderloin, trimmed of visible fat and cut into 1/2-inch thick (12-mm) by 2-inch-long (5-cm) strips

1/2 cup (4 fl oz/125 ml) water

1/3 cup (3 fl oz/80 ml) dry red wine

2 tablespoons balsamic vinegar

6 slices whole wheat (wholemeal) sandwich bread, toasted

♦ In a bowl, combine the arugula and salad greens.

♦ Coat a large nonstick frying pan with nonstick cooking spray. Place over medium-high heat. Add the shallots or onions and mushrooms and sprinkle with half the pepper. Sauté until wilted, 4–5 minutes. Transfer to a bowl.

♦ Increase heat to high. When hot, add the beef and the remaining pepper. Stir-fry, stirring almost constantly, until the meat is browned and fully cooked, 3–4 minutes. Using a slotted spoon, remove the meat.

♦ With the pan still over high heat, add the water, wine, and vinegar. Boil rapidly, stirring to scrape any browned bits from the bottom of the pan, for 1–2 minutes.

♦ To serve, divide the bread among individual plates. Top each with an equal amount of the arugula mixture, shallot-mushroom mixture, beef strips, and pan juices.

e **levate your menus** with one or more of these easy-to-make finishing touches. Whether you are preparing a quick weekday breakfast or a leisurely weekend brunch, a lunch to go or an afternoon tea, a casual after-work supper or a special dinner party, the breads, drinks, and desserts in this chapter will turn any meal into a memorable occasion. Every bread recipe offers the opportunity to enjoy whole grains, often enhanced with fruits or vegetables. Plus, each slice or muffin counts as a grain serving. The drinks in this chapter quench the thirst and also cleverly incorporate an abundance of fresh seasonal fruit, including papaya, strawberries, peaches, and melons. With every pleasurable sip, you're closer to meeting the recommended amount of fruit servings. Grains and fruits are also featured prominently in the desserts that conclude the chapter. These fabulous finishes prove just how truly delicious eating well can be.

finishes

Enjoying fruit butters

Fruit butters are made by gently simmering fruit purées until much of their water content evaporates, resulting in intensely flavored spreads that are almost as thick and smooth as softened dairy butter, but with none of its fat. Their name may make them sound as if they're packed with fat and calories, but fruit butters are, in fact, very healthful.

Their consistency makes fruit butters excellent substitutes for butter or oil in baked goods, in which they contribute moisture, rich taste, and texture while also improving the fiber content.

You'll find fruit butters made from apples, pears, and the peaches shown here, shelved along with jams, jellies, and preserves. Read labels to select a brand that has been sweetened with fruit juice rather than with sugar.

Whole wheat biscuits

Indulge in the great taste of rolls made from a combination of whole wheat flour, for heartiness and fiber, and all-purpose flour, that keeps the dough light and airy. You might want to top them with a delicious fruit butter like the peach one featured here.

MAKES: 16 | **PREPARATION:** 10 minutes | **COOKING:** 14 minutes

1 cup (5 oz/155 g) whole wheat (wholemeal) flour

1 cup (5 oz/155 g) all-purpose (plain) flour

1 1/2 tablespoons sugar

1 tablespoon baking powder

1/2 teaspoon cream of tartar

2 tablespoons cold unsalted butter, cut into small pieces

3/4 cup (6 fl oz/180 ml) lowfat evaporated milk

◆ Preheat an oven to 425°F (220°C). To keep the biscuit bottoms from getting too dark, line a baking sheet with aluminum foil.

◆ Into a bowl, sift together the whole wheat flour, all-purpose flour, sugar, baking powder, and cream of tartar. Add the butter and blend it into the dry ingredients until the mixture resembles fine bread crumbs. Add the milk and stir briskly until you have a sticky, shaggy dough.

◆ Turn the dough out onto a generously floured surface and, with floured hands, knead it gently until it is smooth and manageable but still quite soft, about 10 times. Push and pat the dough into a 7- to 8-inch (18- to 20-cm) square about 1/2 inch (12 mm) thick.

◆ To form biscuits, with a long, sharp knife, cut the dough into 4 equal strips. Make 4 more cuts perpendicular to the first, forming 16 square biscuits. Place them just touching one another on the prepared baking sheet.

◆ Bake until lightly browned and risen to about twice their unbaked height, 12–14 minutes. Serve warm.

PER BISCUIT

Calories	93
Kilojoules	390
Protein	3 g
Carbohydrates	16 g
Total Fat	2 g
Saturated Fat	<1 g
Cholesterol	6 mg
Sodium	105 mg
Dietary Fiber	1 g

Tomato and walnut flat bread

Flat bread is something between a crumbly cracker and a crisp biscuit. Once you've mastered the technique, experiment with ingredients to make both sweet and savory snacks. For this version, be sure to use sun-dried tomatoes packed without oil, to enjoy their intense taste without added fat.

SERVES: 8 | **PREPARATION:** 20 minutes | **COOKING:** 20 minutes

2 cups (16 fl oz/500 ml)
  boiling water

4 sun-dried tomatoes
  (not oil-packed)

1/2 cup (2 1/2 oz/75 g)
  whole wheat (wholemeal)
  flour

1/2 cup (2 1/2 oz/75 g)
  all-purpose (plain) flour

1 tablespoon sugar

1/4 teaspoon salt

1/2 teaspoon baking powder

1/4 teaspoon cayenne pepper

1 egg and 1 egg white

2 tablespoons chopped fresh
  thyme or 2 teaspoons
  dried thyme

1/3 cup (1 1/3 oz/40 g) finely
  chopped walnuts

♦ Preheat an oven to 350°F (180°C). Coat a large, heavy baking sheet with nonstick cooking spray.

♦ In a small bowl, pour the boiling water over the tomatoes. Let stand until the tomatoes are slightly soft, 2–3 minutes. Drain and pat dry with paper towels and chop the tomatoes finely.

♦ Into a large bowl, sift together the whole wheat flour, all-purpose flour, sugar, salt, baking powder, and cayenne. Add the egg and egg white and thyme and stir vigorously to combine. The dough will be very stiff at this point. Add the walnuts and chopped tomatoes and work them into the dough.

♦ Turn the dough out onto a lightly floured surface and knead it a few times. Pat and roll into a 10-inch (25-cm) square about 1/4 inch (6 mm) thick. With a sharp knife, cut the dough crosswise into quarters and place the pieces at least 1 inch (2.5 cm) apart on the prepared baking sheet.

♦ Bake for 10 minutes. Turn over and bake until dry and lightly browned, 8–10 minutes longer. Transfer to a wire rack to cool completely.

♦ To serve, break into small, irregular pieces.

nutrition note

Eggs and alternatives

One egg contains more than 200 milligrams of cholesterol, which is about two thirds of the recommended daily limit for healthy adults. To control your cholesterol intake, limit egg yolks to 4 per week and consider alternatives.

Because all of an egg's fat and cholesterol is contained in its yolk, substitute egg whites for whole eggs when baking. A culinary rule of thumb for established recipes is to substitute whites for whole eggs one-to-one after the first egg. For example, if a recipe calls for 3 eggs, use 1 egg and 2 egg whites instead.

Frozen or refrigerated pasteurized egg products are made commercially from egg whites with added flavorings and, sometimes, vegetable fat to simulate the taste of whole eggs. Depending on the brand, egg products may have less than half the fat of an egg to no fat; all brands are cholesterol-free. Use 1/4 cup (2 fl oz/60 ml) egg product in place of each whole egg.

PER SERVING

Calories	120
Kilojoules	503
Protein	5 g
Carbohydrates	19 g
Total Fat	3 g
Saturated Fat	0 g
Cholesterol	27 mg
Sodium	123 mg
Dietary Fiber	3 g

Spiced muffins with Golden applesauce

Substituting applesauce for oil is a wonderful way to lower fat and add fiber while still producing moist, tasty muffins. Making your own applesauce is an excellent way to use fruit that is too soft for eating out of hand, although firm apples may be used as well.

MAKES: 12 | **PREPARATION:** 10 minutes | **COOKING:** 15 minutes

1½ cups (7½ oz/235 g) whole wheat (wholemeal) flour

½ cup (1½ oz/45 g) rye flour

2 teaspoons ground cardamom

2 teaspoons baking powder

½ teaspoon baking soda (bicarbonate of soda)

¼ cup (¾ oz/20 g) nonfat dry milk

1 cup (8 fl oz/250 ml) Golden Applesauce (recipe follows)

½ cup (4 fl oz/125 ml) water

½ cup (3½ oz/105 g) firmly packed brown sugar

1 egg

2 tablespoons canola oil

1 cup (6 oz/185 g) raisins

♦ Preheat an oven to 375°F (190°C). Coat 12 standard muffin cups with nonstick cooking spray.

♦ Into a medium bowl, sift together the whole wheat flour, rye flour, cardamom, baking powder, and baking soda. Add the dry milk and stir to blend.

♦ In a large bowl, whisk together the applesauce, water, brown sugar, egg, and oil. Add the combined dry ingredients and stir just until the batter is blended. Stir in the raisins. Fill each prepared cup three-quarters full.

♦ Bake until a toothpick inserted in the center of a muffin comes out clean, about 15 minutes. Cool in the cups for 5 minutes before serving.

Golden applesauce

MAKES: 3 cups (24 fl oz/750 ml) | **PREPARATION:** 5 minutes | **COOKING:** 15 minutes

2 lb (1 kg) Golden Delicious apples, cored and cut into 1-inch (2.5-cm) chunks

¼ cup (2 fl oz/60 ml) thawed unsweetened apple juice concentrate

¼ cup (2 fl oz/60 ml) water

2 tablespoons lemon juice

½ teaspoon ground cinnamon

♦ In a large saucepan over high heat, bring the apples, juice concentrate, and water to a boil. Reduce heat to medium, cover, and cook, stirring occasionally, until the apples are mushy, about 15 minutes. Add the lemon juice and cinnamon. Using a potato masher, mash until smooth, or leave lumps if you like a chunky sauce. Serve hot or cold. If not using immediately, cool and refrigerate in a tightly covered container for up to 4 days.

Cranberry and oat muffins

The popular breakfast combination of oatmeal and cranberries is used here in muffins that make an excellent morning bread. A smart way to add grains and fruit to your day is to make, bake, and take along your own snacks rather than stopping for a bakery's high-fat goods.

MAKES: 18 | **PREPARATION:** 10 minutes + 30 minutes soaking | **COOKING:** 15 minutes

2 cups (16 fl oz/500 ml) lowfat buttermilk

1 cup (3 oz/90 g) old-fashioned rolled oats

1 cup (4 oz/125 g) dried cranberries

1²/₃ cups (9 oz/280 g) whole wheat (wholemeal) flour

2 teaspoons ground nutmeg

1 teaspoon baking soda (bicarbonate of soda)

1 teaspoon baking powder

1 egg and 1 egg white

2 tablespoons canola oil

¹/₂ cup (3¹/₂ oz/105 g) firmly packed brown sugar

1 cup (6 oz/185 g) dried currants

¹/₄ cup (2 oz/60 g) granulated sugar

1 teaspoon ground cinnamon

◆ In a large bowl, stir together the buttermilk, oats, and cranberries. Let stand for 30 minutes to plump the cranberries and moisten the oats.

◆ Preheat an oven to 400°F (200°C). Coat 18 standard muffin cups with nonstick cooking spray.

◆ Into a medium bowl, sift together the whole wheat flour, nutmeg, baking soda, and baking powder.

◆ To the buttermilk mixture, add the egg and egg white, oil, brown sugar, and currants and beat until blended. Add the dry ingredients and stir just until combined.

◆ Fill each prepared cup three-quarters full.

◆ In a small bowl, stir together the granulated sugar and cinnamon. Sprinkle an equal amount over each cup of batter.

◆ Bake until a toothpick inserted in the center of a muffin comes out clean, about 15 minutes. Cool in the cups for 5 minutes before serving.

nutrition note

Oats

From Attila the Hun's barbarian hordes to Scottish Highlanders to modern-day body builders, men of strength have long acclaimed the power that eating oats can give.

High in complex carbohydrates and very filling, this nutty-tasting cereal grain is a great source of energy and soluble fiber. Soluble fiber may help lower your blood cholesterol when you include oats in a lowfat diet.

Oats are first processed by removing their inedible hulls, leaving their bran and germ intact. Widely available old-fashioned rolled oats, which are used in recipes in this book, are whole oats that have been steamed until slightly soft, then flattened between steel rollers into disc shapes. Quick-cooking oatmeal is made by cutting the oats into smaller pieces, steaming them, then rolling them even thinner.

PER MUFFIN

Calories	180
Kilojoules	755
Protein	5 g
Carbohydrates	35 g
Total Fat	3 g
Saturated Fat	<1 g
Cholesterol	13 mg
Sodium	146 mg
Dietary Fiber	3 g

Quick brown bread

Cornmeal, whole wheat flour, and rye flour give this dark, moist loaf an earthy, satisfying flavor. This is a faster, oven-baked version of steamed Boston brown bread. To make as muffins, bake the batter in 12 standard-sized muffin cups for 15 minutes.

MAKES: 1 loaf | **SERVES:** 10 | **PREPARATION:** 10 minutes | **COOKING:** 50 minutes

2/3 cup (2 oz/60 g) rye flour

2/3 cup (4 oz/125 g) whole wheat (wholemeal) flour

1/2 cup (2 1/2 oz/75 g) cornmeal (maize flour)

2 teaspoons baking soda (bicarbonate of soda)

1 cup (8 fl oz/250 ml) lowfat buttermilk

1/3 cup (3 1/2 oz/105 g) molasses

1/3 cup (3 fl oz/80 ml) Prune Purée (recipe follows)

1 egg

2/3 cup (4 oz/125 g) raisins

♦ Preheat an oven to 400°F (200°C). Coat a medium (8 1/2-inch/21-cm) loaf pan with nonstick cooking spray.

♦ Into a large bowl, sift together the rye flour, whole wheat flour, cornmeal, and baking soda.

♦ In a medium bowl, whisk together the buttermilk, molasses, prune purée, and egg until smooth.

♦ Add the buttermilk mixture to the dry ingredients and stir just until blended; the batter will be quite thin. Stir in the raisins. Pour into the prepared pan.

♦ Bake until the loaf has risen to the top of the pan and a skewer inserted in the center comes out with just a few moist crumbs on it, 45–50 minutes.

♦ Cool in the pan for 10 minutes before serving.

Prune purée

When substituted for an equal amount of vegetable oil, prune purée contributes flavor and texture to baked recipes. There are several commercial brands available, look for them in the baking section of a well-stocked food store. You can also use puréed prunes sold as baby food.

MAKES: 1/3 cup (3 fl oz/80 ml) | **COOKING:** 30 minutes

1/3 cup (3 oz/90 g) pitted prunes

♦ Put the prunes in a small saucepan and add water to cover. Place over low heat, and simmer gently until the prunes are plump and tender, about 30 minutes. Cool. Place in a food processor and process until smooth.

Multigrain quick bread

Look for both kasha and seven-grain cereal in the bulk-food section or packaged in the cereal section of most supermarkets and natural foods stores. If you can't find seven-grain cereal, substitute an equal amount of old-fashioned rolled oats. Pair with sliced tomatoes and cucumbers.

MAKES: 1 loaf | **SERVES:** 10 | **PREPARATION:** 10 minutes | **COOKING:** 55 minutes

1 cup (5 oz/155 g) whole wheat (wholemeal) flour

3/4 cup (4 oz/125 g) all-purpose (plain) flour

1½ teaspoons baking powder

1 teaspoon ground nutmeg

½ teaspoon ground allspice

1/3 cup (2½ oz/75 g) firmly packed brown sugar

1/4 cup (1 oz/30 g) finely chopped walnuts

½ cup (3 oz/90 g) seven-grain cereal

1/4 cup (2 oz/60 g) kasha, medium granulation

1¼ cups (10 fl oz/310 ml) nonfat milk

1/4 cup (2 fl oz/60 ml) Prune Purée (recipe on page 236)

1 egg and 1 egg white

♦ Preheat an oven to 375°F (190°C). Coat a medium (8½-inch/21-cm) loaf pan with nonstick cooking spray.

♦ Into a medium bowl, sift together the whole wheat flour, all-purpose flour, baking powder, nutmeg, and allspice. Add the brown sugar, walnuts, seven-grain cereal, and kasha. Toss to combine.

♦ In a small bowl, whisk together the milk, prune purée, and egg and egg white. Add the milk mixture to the combined dry ingredients and stir just until blended. Pour into the prepared pan.

♦ Bake until a skewer inserted in the center of the loaf comes out clean, 50–55 minutes.

♦ Cool in the pan for 10 minutes before serving.

nutrition note

Flours and fiber

Baked goods are an excellent way to get your daily servings of grains, especially when they include flours milled from whole grains. As illustrated here, whole grain flours contain considerably more fiber than does all-purpose (plain) flour. For a guide to using various whole grain flours in recipes, see page 243.

Per 1 cup (5 oz/155 g):

FLOUR	FIBER
All-purpose (plain)	3 g
Buckwheat	12 g
Whole grain cornmeal	9 g
Rye (light/medium)	15 g
Whole wheat (wholemeal)	15 g

PER SERVING

Calories	223
Kilojoules	935
Protein	7 g
Carbohydrates	42 g
Total Fat	4 g
Saturated Fat	<1 g
Cholesterol	22 mg
Sodium	106 mg
Dietary Fiber	3 g

Cooking pumpkin

Canned pumpkin purée, available year-round, is an easy source for the mashed cooked pumpkin called for in this recipe. When pumpkins abound in markets during autumn, however, you may want to make your own purée.

• *Look for whole "pie" or "sugar" pumpkins that weigh 6 pounds (3 kg) or less, or buy cut pieces of larger pumpkins.*

• *With a large, sturdy, sharp knife, carefully cut whole pumpkins in half, and use a sharp-edged spoon to scoop and scrape out the seeds and fibers from the inside.*

• *Put the halves or pieces, shell side up, in a baking dish and pour in water to come about 1 inch (2.5 cm) up the sides. Bake in a 375°F (190°C) oven until tender, 45 minutes to 1 hour.*

• *When cool enough to handle, scoop the pulp from the shells and mash with a potato masher or purée in a blender or food processor. Use now, or refrigerate in a tightly covered container for up to 3 days.*

PER SERVING

Calories	200
Kilojoules	837
Protein	4 g
Carbohydrates	42 g
Total Fat	3 g
Saturated Fat	<1 g
Cholesterol	21 mg
Sodium	175 mg
Dietary Fiber	3 g

Spicy pumpkin ginger bread

When the sweetness of pumpkin pie is too much after a large holiday meal, consider this savory bread instead. Note that this recipe makes 2 loaves, which makes it a great choice for feeding a crowd or to give as gifts. Don't be intimidated by the long list of ingredients: This bread mixes up quickly.

MAKES: 2 loaves | **SERVES:** 20 | **PREPARATION:** 15 minutes | **COOKING:** 1 hour

2 cups (10 oz/315 g) whole wheat (wholemeal) flour

1/2 cup (2 1/2 oz/75 g) oat flour or oat bran

1/2 cup (2 1/2 oz/75 g) cornmeal (maize flour)

2 teaspoons baking soda (bicarbonate of soda)

1 teaspoon baking powder

2 teaspoons ground ginger

1 teaspoon ground cinnamon

1 teaspoon ground nutmeg

2 cups (1 lb/500 g) mashed cooked pumpkin or canned unseasoned pumpkin purée

1 1/2 cups (10 1/2 oz/330 g) firmly packed brown sugar

2 eggs and 3 egg whites

2/3 cup (5 fl oz/160 ml) water

1/2 cup (4 fl oz/125 ml) Prune Purée (recipe on page 236)

2 tablespoons canola oil

1/2 cup (3 oz/90 g) chopped dried pears

1/2 cup (3 oz/90 g) golden raisins (sultanas)

1/2 cup (1 oz/30 g) chopped candied ginger

♦ Preheat an oven to 350°F (180°C). Coat two medium (8 1/2-inch/21-cm) loaf pans with nonstick cooking spray.

♦ Into a medium bowl, sift together the whole wheat flour, oat flour or bran, cornmeal, baking soda, baking powder, ground ginger, cinnamon, and nutmeg.

♦ In a large bowl, whisk together the pumpkin, brown sugar, eggs and egg whites, water, prune purée, and oil until smooth. Add the combined dry ingredients and beat just until blended. Stir in the pears, raisins, and candied ginger. Divide the batter evenly between the prepared pans.

♦ Bake until a skewer inserted in the center of the loaves comes out clean, about 1 hour.

♦ Cool in the pans for 10 minutes before serving.

Herbed whole wheat popovers

Popovers bake up best in individual glass custard cups or ceramic ramekins. Well-seasoned cast-iron popover pans, if you have them, are also good. If using a standard-sized muffin tin, fill the cups around the outside of the tin only, as popovers in interior cups won't rise properly.

MAKES: 8 | **PREPARATION:** 5 minutes | **COOKING:** 30 minutes

1 egg and 2 egg whites

1 tablespoon canola oil

1½ cups (12 fl oz/375 ml) nonfat milk

1 teaspoon dried basil

⅛ teaspoon cayenne pepper

1 cup (5 oz/155 g) whole wheat (wholemeal) flour

½ cup (2½ oz/75 g) all-purpose (plain) flour

♦ Preheat an oven to 450°F (230°C). Generously coat 8 individual ramekins, 4–fl oz (125–ml) custard cups, or standard muffin cups with nonstick cooking spray. If using ramekins or custard cups, set them on a baking sheet for easier handling. If using muffin cups, pour 2 tablespoons water into each interior cup of the pan to temper the heat.

♦ In a bowl, whisk together the egg and egg whites, oil, milk, basil, and cayenne until blended. Add the whole wheat flour and all-purpose flour and whisk until completely smooth and free of any lumps. Alternatively, the batter can be mixed in a blender or food processor.

♦ Fill each prepared cup one-half to two-thirds full. Bake until the popovers are well browned and have puffed dramatically, about 30 minutes.

♦ Remove from the oven and immediately lift the popovers carefully from their cups. Serve immediately, as popovers tend to deflate quickly.

cooking clinic

Substituting flours

Whole grain flours, including those made from buckwheat, whole grain cornmeal, rye, and whole wheat (wholemeal), provide more fiber than all-purpose (plain) flour (see page 239). They also present a dense texture in baked goods.

The recipes in this book have been tested to make sure that the baked item is not too coarse or strongly flavored. A good rule of thumb for using whole grain flours in established recipes is to begin by substituting just one-third of the all-purpose flour until you are sure of the results of your switch.

PER POPOVER

Calories	140
Kilojoules	586
Protein	7 g
Carbohydrates	22 g
Total Fat	3 g
Saturated Fat	<1 g
Cholesterol	27 mg
Sodium	47 mg
Dietary Fiber	2 g

Sunshine juice blend

Wheat germ, the embryo of the wheat kernel, which is separated during milling, abounds in fiber. The strawberries and peaches add more fiber plus vitamin C, making this fruit-filled drink a wonderful way to start the day or finish a meal.

SERVES: 2 | **PREPARATION:** 5 minutes

2 cups (8 oz/250 g) hulled fresh strawberries

1 peach, peeled, pitted, and coarsely chopped

1/2 cup (4 fl oz/125 ml) nonfat milk

2 tablespoons wheat germ

1 tablespoon honey

3 ice cubes

♦ In a blender, combine the strawberries, peach, milk, wheat germ, honey, and ice cubes. Blend until smooth, about 20 seconds.

♦ To serve, divide between glasses.

Papaya agua fresca

Agua fresca, Spanish for "fresh water," is a popular Mexican drink that is wonderfully refreshing on a hot day. Make it with a variety of peeled and seeded fresh fruits, including strawberry, watermelon, kiwifruit, or mango, or unsweetened frozen fruit.

SERVES: 2 | **PREPARATION:** 5 minutes

1 large papaya (1 1/4 lb/625 g), peeled, halved, seeded, and cut into chunks

2 tablespoons lime juice

1 1/2 cups (12 fl oz/375 ml) carbonated water

♦ In a blender or food processor, process the papaya and lime juice until smooth. You will have 1 cup (8 fl oz/ 250 ml) fruit purée.

♦ To serve, divide the water between ice-filled glasses. Add the fruit purée and stir to mix well.

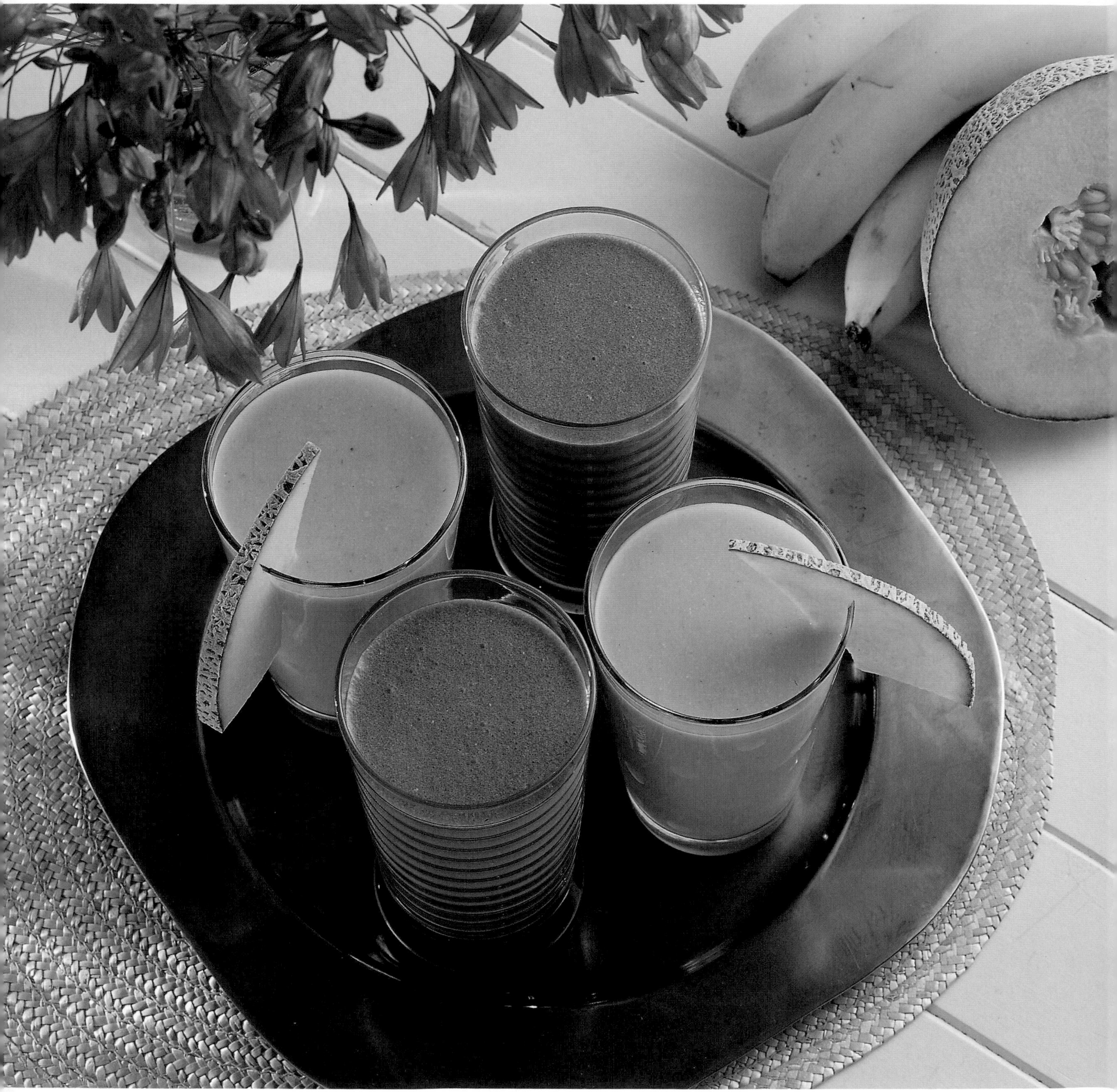

Cantaloupe smoothie

Delicious cantaloupes are one of the most nutrient-rich foods you can eat. Start your morning with this lowfat, reduced-sodium drink combination and you'll have much of the vitamins A and C you need for the entire day.

SERVES: 2 | **PREPARATION:** 5 minutes

1/2 cantaloupe, seeded, peeled, and cut into chunks

1 banana, cut into pieces

1/3 cup (3 fl oz/80 ml) orange juice

1/4 cup (2 oz/60 g) plain nonfat yogurt

1 tablespoon 100% unprocessed wheat bran

◆ In a blender, combine the cantaloupe, banana, orange juice, yogurt, and wheat bran. Blend until smooth, about 20 seconds.

◆ To serve, divide between glasses.

PER SERVING

Calories	138
Kilojoules	576
Protein	4 g
Carbohydrates	32 g
Total Fat	<1 g
Saturated Fat	<1 g
Cholesterol	<1 mg
Sodium	35 mg
Dietary Fiber	3 g

Banana-chocolate shake

To give this shake a fluffy texture, choose firm but ripe bananas, then peel and freeze them for at least 1 hour—or as long as overnight—before blending the drinks. Because each serving contains so much milk, this shake is a delicious way to boost calcium.

SERVES: 2 | **PREPARATION:** 3 minutes

2 large bananas, cut into pieces

2 cups (16 fl oz/500 ml) cold nonfat milk

1 teaspoon vanilla extract (essence)

2 tablepoons unsweetened cocoa powder

◆ In a blender, combine the bananas, milk, vanilla, and cocoa powder. Blend until light and frothy, about 30 seconds.

◆ To serve, divide between glasses.

PER SERVING

Calories	224
Kilojoules	940
Protein	11 g
Carbohydrates	46 g
Total Fat	2 g
Saturated Fat	<1 g
Cholesterol	5 mg
Sodium	130 mg
Dietary Fiber	4 g

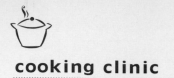

Thickening naturally

Use these flavorless products, found in the baking sections of most markets, to contribute body to dishes without adding fat:

Gelatin. *Unflavored gelatin is sold in individual packets containing 1/4 ounce (about 1 tablespoon) each with the thickening power to set about 2 cups (16 fl oz/500 ml) of liquid to a firm gel.*

Pectin. *Extracted from the cores, seeds, and skins of various fruits, this substance is often used for making jellies and jams. You can also use it to lend body to salad dressings.*

Tapioca. *This highly digestible starchy powder is made from the root of the tropical cassava plant, also known as manioc. Purchase it as tiny, ball-shaped "pearl" tapioca or as quicker-cooking, finely ground flakes or powder. Use tapioca to thicken dishes as diverse as soups, puddings, and pie fillings.*

PER SERVING

Calories	200
Kilojoules	836
Protein	9 g
Carbohydrates	40 g
Total Fat	<1 g
Saturated Fat	<1 g
Cholesterol	3 mg
Sodium	116 mg
Dietary Fiber	3 g

Fancy fruit parfaits

Plain yogurt flavored with vanilla and thickened with gelatin becomes a delicate custardlike cream that is good by itself or as a topping for cereal, pancakes, waffles, or fruit. Layering it with fruit in a parfait glass makes a delightful treat to end a meal.

SERVES: 6 | **PREPARATION:** 20 minutes | **COOKING:** 3 minutes | **CHILLING:** 1 1/2 hours

3 cups (1 1/2 lb/750 g) plain nonfat yogurt

1/3 cup (3 oz/90 g) sugar

2 teaspoons grated orange zest

2 teaspoons vanilla extract (essence)

2 teaspoons unflavored gelatin

1/3 cup (3 fl oz/80 ml) nonfat evaporated milk

1 1/2 cups (12 oz/375 g) fresh blackberries

1 cantaloupe, peeled, seeded, and cut into 1/2-inch (12-mm) cubes

♦ In a large bowl, stir together the yogurt, sugar, orange zest, and vanilla until smooth.

♦ In a small, heavy saucepan, sprinkle the gelatin over the evaporated milk. Let stand for 5 minutes to allow the gelatin to soften. Place over low heat and stir constantly until the gelatin dissolves, about 3 minutes. The milk should be hot to the touch, but not come to a boil.

♦ Stir the gelatin mixture into the yogurt mixture. Refrigerate, stirring occasionally, until the mixture is the consistency of softly set pudding, about 1 1/2 hours.

♦ Spoon 1/4 cup (2 oz/60 g) of the yogurt mixture into each of 6 stemmed glasses. Reserve 18 whole berries for garnish. Divide the cantaloupe and remaining berries evenly among the glasses. Top with an equal amount of the remaining yogurt mixture. Serve now, or cover and refrigerate for up to 8 hours.

♦ To serve, garnish with the reserved berries.

Summer fruit cobbler

Flummery, pandowdy, slump, and cobbler are American regional terms for dough-topped fruit desserts. Here, peaches are combined with plums and apricots to increase the ratio of fruit to topping. Use any combination of summer fruits, cut into pieces of about the same size.

SERVES: 6 | **PREPARATION:** 25 minutes | **COOKING:** 40 minutes | **COOLING:** 30 minutes

3 peaches, 1 lb (500 g) total, pitted and sliced

8 apricots, 1 lb (500 g) total, pitted and sliced

6 plums, 1 lb (500 g) total, pitted and sliced

1/4 cup (2 oz/60 g) sugar

2 tablespoons lemon juice

1 tablespoon quick-cooking tapioca powder

1 cup (5 oz/155 g) all-purpose (plain) flour

1 teaspoon baking powder

1/2 teaspoon ground cinnamon

1/2 teaspoon ground nutmeg

1 egg

1/4 cup (2 fl oz/60 ml) nonfat milk

1/4 cup (2 fl oz/60 ml) Golden Applesauce (recipe on page 232)

♦ Preheat an oven to 375°F (190°C). Coat an 8-inch (20-cm) square baking pan with nonstick cooking spray.

♦ In a large bowl, toss the peaches, apricots, and plums with half the sugar, the lemon juice, and tapioca. Spread in the prepared pan.

♦ Into a medium bowl, sift together the flour, baking powder, cinnamon, nutmeg, and the remaining sugar.

♦ In a small bowl, beat together the egg, milk, and applesauce until smooth. Add to the combined dry ingredients and stir just until blended. The batter will be quite stiff. Spoon the batter randomly over the fruit. Do not be concerned with covering the fruit completely, since the batter will spread during baking.

♦ Bake until the topping is well browned and the juices are bubbling around the edge, about 40 minutes. Cool at least 30 minutes before serving. Serve warm or cold.

PER SERVING

Calories	240
Kilojoules	1,008
Protein	6 g
Carbohydrates	53 g
Total Fat	2 g
Saturated Fat	<1 g
Cholesterol	36 mg
Sodium	107 mg
Dietary Fiber	4 g

Chocolate pudding pie

It's hard to resist a chocolate pie, but you don't have to when the pie in question is this low in calories and fat. To save time, put the filling in a purchased crust. However, many of these are higher in fat and lower in dietary fiber than this version.

SERVES: 8 | **PREPARATION:** 30 minutes | **COOKING:** 30 minutes | **CHILLING:** 2 hours

Crust

8 whole graham crackers (wholemeal biscuits)

2/3 cup (2 oz/60 g) 100% unprocessed wheat bran

2 tablespoons sugar

1/4 teaspoon ground cinnamon

2 egg whites

Filling

1/3 cup (1½ oz/45 g) cornstarch (cornflour)

1/3 cup (5 oz/155 g) sugar

1/3 cup (1 oz/30 g) unsweetened cocoa powder

3½ cups (28 fl oz/875 ml) nonfat milk

2 teaspoons vanilla extract (essence)

16 strawberries, hulled

♦ Preheat an oven to 350°F (180°C). Coat a 9-inch (23-cm) pie pan with nonstick cooking spray.

♦ To make the crust, in a food processor, process the graham crackers and wheat bran to fine crumbs. Add the sugar, cinnamon, and egg whites and process just until all the crumbs are dampened.

♦ Put the mixture in the prepared pan and firmly pat and press it over the bottom and sides of the pan, taking care not to make the edges too thick.

♦ Bake until the crust has browned lightly, feels firm but not hard, and gives to moderate pressure, about 15 minutes. If overbaked, it will be brittle when cold. Cool completely, about 1 hour.

♦ To make the filling, into a heavy saucepan, sift together the cornstarch, sugar, and cocoa powder. Gradually whisk in the milk. Place over medium heat and cook, whisking almost constantly, until the mixture thickens and boils, about 7 minutes. Reduce heat to medium-low and boil gently, whisking constantly, 2 minutes longer. Remove from heat and press a piece of plastic wrap directly onto the surface of the mixture to prevent a skin from forming. Cool for 30 minutes.

♦ Remove the plastic wrap from the filling and stir in the vanilla. Pour the filling into the crust and refrigerate until set, at least 2 hours.

♦ To serve, cut into wedges. Garnish with the berries.

Grilled summer fruits with Apricot sauce

Almost all tree fruits adapt well to outdoor grilling. Although you don't need to peel most summer fruits, you may want to peel autumn fruits such as apples and pears before grilling. Grill these firmer fruits about twice as long as the softer summer fruits.

SERVES: 6 | **PREPARATION:** 15 minutes | **COOKING:** 15 minutes

½ cup (4 fl oz/125 ml) thawed unsweetened apple juice concentrate

½ teaspoon ground cinnamon

3 peaches, halved and pitted

6 apricots, halved and pitted

Apricot Sauce (recipe follows)

½ teaspoon ground nutmeg

◆ Prepare a fire in a charcoal grill or preheat a gas grill or broiler (griller). Position the cooking rack 4–6 inches (10–15 cm) from the heat source.

◆ In a small bowl, whisk together the apple juice concentrate and cinnamon.

◆ Arrange the fruit, cut side down, on the rack or broiler pan. Grill or broil, brushing with the juice mixture and turning with a spatula every 2–3 minutes, until the fruit is lightly browned and soft but not mushy, 8–10 minutes total.

◆ To serve, arrange the fruit, cut side up, on individual plates. Top with an equal amount of the sauce. Dust with the nutmeg.

PER SERVING

Calories	146
Kilojoules	612
Protein	4 g
Carbohydrates	34 g
Total Fat	<1 g
Saturated Fat	<1 g
Cholesterol	<1 mg
Sodium	48 mg
Dietary Fiber	2 g

Apricot sauce

MAKES: 1½ cups (12 fl oz/375 ml) | **PREPARATION:** 5 minutes

⅓ cup (3 oz/90 g) apricot jam

1¼ cups (10 oz/315 g) plain nonfat yogurt

2 drops almond extract (essence)

◆ In a small bowl, stir and mash the jam to soften it. Add the yogurt and almond extract and stir until blended. Serve now, or refrigerate in a tightly covered container for up to 3 days.

PER ¼ CUP (2 FL OZ/60 ML)

Calories	61
Kilojoules	255
Protein	3 g
Carbohydrates	13 g
Total Fat	<1 g
Saturated Fat	<1 g
Cholesterol	<1 mg
Sodium	42 mg
Dietary Fiber	<1 g

Freezing fresh berries

Whole berries, including the strawberries used in this recipe, offer home cooks the advantage of being easy to freeze in season for future use. Your freezer must be capable of freezing foods to 0°F (-18°C) and holding them there.

To freeze berries, simply rinse, dry, and hull the berries. Spread them, not touching each other, in a single layer on a baking sheet.

Leave the sheet in the freezer until the berries are frozen solid, about 4 hours. Transfer the berries to a tightly covered container, packing them loosely. They will keep well for 10–12 months.

The same technique may be used to freeze currants or grapes, which will keep for the same length of time.

PER SERVING

Calories	245
Kilojoules	1,027
Protein	5 g
Carbohydrates	53 g
Total Fat	<1 g
Saturated Fat	<1 g
Cholesterol	3 mg
Sodium	47 mg
Dietary Fiber	6 g

Strawberry shiver and kiwi topping

When fresh strawberries fill produce stands, it's tempting to buy entire flats of the beautiful jewels. With this quick method for making an icy dessert, you can indulge in all the strawberries you want. Just freeze the berries—whole or made into this lowfat delight—to enjoy for many weeks.

SERVES: 4 | **PREPARATION:** 20 minutes | **FREEZING:** 4 hours (for fresh berries)

4 cups (1 lb/500 g) hulled fresh strawberries or frozen unsweetened whole strawberries

1 tablespoon lemon juice

1/2 cup (4 fl oz/125 ml) nonfat sweetened condensed milk

Kiwi Topping

5 kiwifruits, peeled

2 tablespoons water

2 tablespoons sugar

2 tablespoons tequila

♦ If using fresh strawberries, spread them on a baking sheet and place in the freezer until frozen solid, at least 4 hours. If using commercially frozen berries, be sure that they, too, are frozen solid.

♦ In a food processor, process the berries until they form very fine, icy shards, 1–1 1/2 minutes. About every 30 seconds, stop the machine to scrape down the sides of the container and push the berries into the blades. Make sure the berries are processed finely, or the finished mixture will have tiny lumps.

♦ Add the lemon juice and condensed milk and process until the mixture is smooth and pale pink, 2–3 minutes, stopping about every 30 seconds to scrape down the sides of the container and push the mixture into the blades. Serve now, or freeze in a tightly covered container for up to 1 week.

♦ To make the kiwi topping, cut 4 of the kiwifruit into chunks. In a blender or food processor, purée the kiwis and water until smooth. Scrape the mixture into a bowl. Add the sugar and tequila and stir until the sugar dissolves. Serve now, or refrigerate in a tightly covered container for up to 3 days. Slice the remaining kiwi.

♦ To serve, divide the shiver among individual bowls. Top each with an equal amount of the kiwi topping. Garnish with the kiwi slices.

Buckwheat and apricot cake

A cross between a cake and a bread, this wheat-filled treat makes a delightful accompaniment to a cup of herb tea. Enjoy it as part of teatime, an old-fashioned tradition that offers a welcome change of pace on an especially hectic day.

SERVES: 8 | **PREPARATION:** 10 minutes + 15 minutes soaking | **COOKING:** 35 minutes

⅓ cup (2 oz/60 g) bulgur wheat

⅓ cup (3 fl oz/80 ml) water

¾ cup (3 oz/90 g) buckwheat flour

¾ cup (3 oz/90 g) all-purpose (plain) flour

1 teaspoon baking powder

1 teaspoon baking soda (bicarbonate of soda)

½ teaspoon ground cloves

1 teaspoon ground cinnamon

¾ cup (6 fl oz/180 ml) lowfat buttermilk

⅓ cup (4 oz/125 g) honey

1 egg

¼ cup (2 fl oz/60 ml) Prune Purée (recipe on page 236)

½ cup (3 oz/90 g) chopped dried apricots

1 tablespoon grated lemon zest

◆ In a large bowl, stir together the bulgur wheat and water. Let stand for 15 minutes.

◆ Preheat an oven to 375°F (190°C). Coat a 9-inch (23-cm) round cake pan with nonstick cooking spray.

◆ Into a medium bowl, sift together the buckwheat flour, all-purpose flour, baking powder, baking soda, cloves, and cinnamon.

◆ To the bulgur mixture, add the buttermilk, honey, egg, prune purée, and apricots and beat until blended. Stir in the combined dry ingredients. Spread in the prepared pan.

◆ Bake until a skewer inserted in the center comes out clean, about 35 minutes.

◆ Cool in the pan for 10 minutes before serving. Top with the lemon zest.

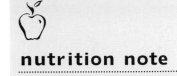

nutrition note

Dried fruit

Dried fruit, such as the apricots in this quick bread, offer yet another enjoyable way to incorporate fruit for eating well. Like fresh fruit, they provide plentiful amounts of nutrients and fiber with virtually no fat or sodium. Because they are greatly reduced in size through the drying process, they are, weight for weight, much higher in calories than fresh fruit.

The recipes in this book allow you to enjoy the intense flavor and chewy texture of dried fruit by making a little go a long way.

Per ½ cup (3 oz/90 g):

FRUIT	CALORIES (KILOJOULES)
Fresh apricots	55 (231)
Dried apricots	265 (1,113)

PER SERVING

Calories	201
Kilojoules	843
Protein	5 g
Carbohydrates	44 g
Total Fat	1 g
Saturated Fat	<1 g
Cholesterol	28 mg
Sodium	263 mg
Dietary Fiber	4 g

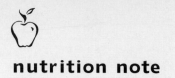
Tropical-fruit crisps

By following these guidelines for preparing fruit and topping, you can transform almost any seasonal fruit into a crisp. In this recipe, some of the shiny black papaya seeds are added, giving a crunchy texture and an interesting spiciness to this warm concoction.

SERVES: 6 | **PREPARATION:** 20 minutes | **COOKING:** 45 minutes | **COOLING:** 30 minutes

2 papayas

2 mangoes

2 tablespoons granulated sugar

2 tablespoons lemon juice

1 tablespoon tapioca flour or quick-cooking tapioca powder

1 teaspoon ground cardamom

1 cup (3 oz/90 g) old-fashioned rolled oats

2 slices whole wheat (wholemeal) sandwich bread, made into crumbs (see page 79)

¼ cup (2 oz/60 g) brown sugar

½ teaspoon ground nutmeg

1 teaspoon vanilla extract (essence)

1 tablespoon unsalted butter, melted

♦ Preheat an oven to 350°F (180°C). Coat an 8-inch (20-cm) square baking pan with nonstick cooking spray.

♦ Peel and halve the papayas. Scoop out 2 tablespoons of the papaya seeds and place them in a large bowl; discard the remaining seeds. Cut the papayas into 1-inch (2.5-cm) cubes and place in the bowl with the seeds.

♦ Peel the mangoes. Using a sharp knife, cut the fruit of the mangoes from the fibrous pit into long strips. Cut the strips into 1-inch-long (2.5-cm) pieces and add them to the bowl with the papayas.

♦ Add the granulated sugar, lemon juice, tapioca, and cardamom and toss to coat the fruit evenly.

♦ In a medium bowl, combine the oats, bread crumbs, brown sugar, nutmeg, and vanilla. Stir until the mixture is crumbly.

♦ Spread half the oat mixture in the prepared pan. Add the fruit mixture. Stir together the butter and oat mixture remaining in the bowl. Spread over the fruit.

♦ Bake until the topping has browned and the fruit is tender, 40–45 minutes. Cool at least 30 minutes before serving. Serve warm or cold.

Dutch apple pancake

Serve this traditional Dutch pancake for breakfast as well as dessert. It is essential that you put the batter into the pans before the apples. If you add the fruit first, the pancakes will puff to only a fraction of their potential. This recipe is best served piping hot.

MAKES: 2 pancakes | **SERVES:** 4 | **PREPARATION:** 15 minutes | **COOKING:** 30 minutes

4 Golden Delicious apples, halved, cored, and cut into 1/4-inch-thick (6-mm) slices

3 tablespoons honey or maple syrup

1/2 teaspoon ground cinnamon

1/4 teaspoon ground nutmeg

2 eggs and 2 egg whites

1/2 cup (4 fl oz/125 ml) nonfat milk

1 tablespoon canola oil

1 teaspoon vanilla extract (essence)

1 tablespoon grated orange zest

1/4 cup (1 1/2 oz/45 g) all-purpose (plain) flour

1/4 cup (1 1/2 oz/45 g) whole wheat (wholemeal) flour

1 tablespoon confectioners' (icing) sugar

4 lemon wedges

♦ Preheat an oven to 425°F (220°C). Coat two 9-inch (23-cm) pie pans with nonstick cooking spray.

♦ Coat a large nonstick frying pan with nonstick cooking spray and place over medium heat. Add the apple slices and cook, stirring and tossing every 2–3 minutes, until they have softened slightly and are browned in spots, about 10 minutes.

♦ Add the honey or syrup, cinnamon, and nutmeg and continue cooking, stirring frequently, until the apples are tender and the honey coats them in a syrupy glaze, about 5 minutes.

♦ In a bowl, beat the eggs and egg whites, milk, oil, vanilla, and orange zest until blended. Add the all-purpose flour and whole wheat flour and beat until completely smooth.

♦ Divide the batter evenly between the prepared pans. Top each with an equal amount of the apple slices.

♦ Bake until golden brown and puffed, about 20 minutes. Remove from the oven and dust with the confectioners' sugar. Cut each pancake in half and serve immediately. Pass the lemon wedges at the table.

PER SERVING

Calories	282
Kilojoules	1,180
Protein	9 g
Carbohydrates	48 g
Total Fat	7 g
Saturated Fat	1 g
Cholesterol	107 mg
Sodium	77 mg
Dietary Fiber	4 g

Baked cinnamon pears with Yogurt cheese

These elegantly presented baked globes hide a fruit filling packed with nutrients and fiber. Yogurt Cheese makes a nice lowfat alternative to whipped cream. Note that only yogurt produced without gum additives or stabilizers will drain properly.

SERVES: 4 | **PREPARATION:** 20 minutes | **COOKING:** 40 minutes

2 tablespoons firmly packed brown sugar

2 tablespoons Prune Purée (recipe on page 236)

1/4 cup (1 1/2 oz/45 g) raisins

1/4 cup (1 1/2 oz/45 g) finely chopped dates

1 teaspoon finely grated lemon zest

1/2 teaspoon ground cinnamon

4 large Bosc pears

1/2 cup (4 fl oz/125 ml) water

1 cinnamon stick, broken

Yogurt Cheese (recipe follows)

♦ Preheat an oven to 325°F (165°C).

♦ In a small bowl, mash together the brown sugar, prune purée, raisins, dates, lemon zest, and cinnamon until they form a damp, gritty paste.

♦ Keeping the stem and stem end intact, peel and core the pears, digging out a cavity 1 inch (2.5 cm) across and 2 1/2 inches (6 cm) deep from the center of the large, or blossom, end.

♦ Divide the brown sugar mixture evenly among the pears, pressing the mixture firmly into each cavity.

♦ Set the pears, stems up, in a baking pan just large enough to hold them. Add the water and cinnamon stick to the pan and cover snugly with aluminum foil.

♦ Bake until the pears are tender, about 40 minutes.

♦ To serve, transfer the pears to individual plates. Top each with an equal amount of the pan juices. Place an equal amount of yogurt cheese next to each pear. Serve warm or cold.

PER SERVING

Calories	224
Kilojoules	936
Protein	4 g
Carbohydrates	55 g
Total Fat	<1 g
Saturated Fat	<1 g
Cholesterol	0 mg
Sodium	25 mg
Dietary Fiber	6 g

Yogurt cheese

MAKES: 1/2 cup (4 oz/125 g) | **PREPARATION:** 5 minutes | **DRAINING:** 8 hours

1 cup (8 oz/250 g) plain nonfat yogurt, without gum additives or stabilizers

♦ Set a fine-mesh sieve or larger-mesh sieve lined with a paper coffee filter over a bowl. Without stirring the yogurt, gently spoon it into the sieve. Place in the refrigerator to drain for 8 hours. Discard or drink the tangy liquid in the bowl. Serve now, or refrigerate in a tightly covered container for up to 1 week.

PER TABLESPOON

Calories	40
Kilojoules	167
Protein	4 g
Carbohydrates	4 g
Total Fat	0 g
Saturated Fat	0 g
Cholesterol	0 mg
Sodium	40 mg
Dietary Fiber	0 g

Roasted pineapple with Raspberry sauce

When choosing a pineapple, tug on a leaf at the center of its crown. If it plucks out easily, you've found a ripe one. Because the Raspberry Sauce can be made from frozen berries, it is a wonderful year-round alternative to syrup for pancakes, frozen yogurt, or angel food cake.

SERVES: 6 | **PREPARATION:** 10 minutes | **COOKING:** 30 minutes

1 pineapple

1/3 cup (3 fl oz/80 ml) rum

1/4 cup (2 oz/60 g) firmly packed brown sugar

1/2 teaspoon ground nutmeg

1 1/2 cups (12 fl oz/375 ml) Raspberry Sauce (recipe follows)

6 mint sprigs

◆ Preheat an oven to 400°F (200°C). Coat a glass 13 x 9-inch (33 x 23-cm) baking pan with nonstick cooking spray.

◆ Peel, quarter, and core the pineapple. Cut each quarter lengthwise into thirds and then crosswise in half. Place the spears into the prepared pan. Sprinkle with the rum, brown sugar, and nutmeg. Stir and toss to coat the pineapple evenly.

◆ Bake, stirring every 10 minutes, until the pineapple is tender and the pan juices have mostly evaporated, about 30 minutes.

◆ To serve, place an equal amount of the sauce on individual plates. Top with an equal number of the pineapple spears. Garnish with a mint sprig.

PER SERVING

Calories	124
Kilojoules	520
Protein	1 g
Carbohydrates	31 g
Total Fat	<1 g
Saturated Fat	<1 g
Cholesterol	0 mg
Sodium	5 mg
Dietary Fiber	3 g

Raspberry sauce

MAKES: 2 cups (16 fl oz/500 ml) | **PREPARATION:** 5 minutes

2 1/2 cups (10 oz/315 g) fresh raspberries or frozen sweetened raspberries, thawed

1/3 cup (3 fl oz/80 ml) water

1 tablespoon lemon juice

2 tablespoons sugar

◆ In a blender or food processor, process the raspberries with the water. Place a fine-mesh sieve over a small bowl and strain to remove the seeds. Add the lemon juice and sugar and stir until the sugar dissolves. Fresh raspberries may need additional sugar. Serve now, or refrigerate in a tightly covered container for up to 5 days.

PER 1/4 CUP (2 FL OZ/60 ML)

Calories	30
Kilojoules	125
Protein	0 g
Carbohydrates	7 g
Total Fat	0 g
Saturated Fat	0 g
Cholesterol	0 mg
Sodium	0 mg
Dietary Fiber	2 g

Zesting citrus

The colorful outermost layer of a citrus fruit's peel, the zest is full of essential oils that contribute lively flavor and aroma to both sweet and savory dishes.

Remove the zest by grating it with the fine rasps of a hand-held grater to form fine particles that blend well with other ingredients. Alternatively, cut it into thin strips with the sharp-edged holes of a special hand-held tool known as a citrus zester. Or remove the zest with a swivel-bladed vegetable peeler before cutting or chopping it into pieces of the desired shape and fineness.

Whatever method you use, always rinse the citrus fruit under cold running water and dry it with a kitchen towel beforehand. Take care not to remove any of the bitter white pith beneath the zest.

PER COOKIE

Calories	60
Kilojoules	249
Protein	2 g
Carbohydrates	14 g
Total Fat	<1 g
Saturated Fat	0 g
Cholesterol	0 mg
Sodium	18 mg
Dietary Fiber	1 g

Cherry tea cookies

This crunchy, twice-baked dunking cookie is ideal for dipping in coffee, tea, milk, or sweet wine. Although baking evaporates some of the alcohol from the rum, to make these cookies alcohol-free, use rum extract rather than rum.

MAKES: 40 | **PREPARATION:** 30 minutes | **COOKING:** 45 minutes | **COOLING:** 20 minutes

1 cup (4 oz/125 g) chopped dried cherries

1/3 cup (3 fl oz/80 ml) rum

13/4 cups (9 oz/280 g) all-purpose (plain) flour

1 cup (5 oz/155 g) whole wheat (wholemeal) flour

2/3 cup (5 oz/155 g) sugar

1 teaspoon baking powder

1 teaspoon ground cinnamon

1 cup (21/2 oz/80 g) 100% unprocessed wheat bran

4 egg whites

1 tablespoon grated orange zest

11/2 teaspoons vanilla extract (essence)

1/2 teaspoon almond extract (essence)

◆ In a small saucepan over medium heat, bring the cherries and rum to a simmer. Cover and remove from heat for 10 minutes. Uncover and cool for 10 minutes longer.

◆ Preheat an oven to 350°F (180°C). Cover a large baking sheet with aluminum foil and coat the foil with nonstick cooking spray.

◆ Into a large bowl, sift together the all-purpose flour, whole wheat flour, sugar, baking powder, and cinnamon. Stir in the wheat bran.

◆ In a small bowl, whisk together the egg whites, orange zest, and vanilla and almond extracts until smooth. Add the cherry and rum mixture and whisk to combine. Add to the combined dry ingredients. Stir to combine into a cohesive mass.

◆ Turn the dough out onto a generously floured work surface and divide in half. Flour each half and shape into a log about 3 inches (7.5 cm) across and 15 inches (38 cm) long. Place the logs on the prepared sheet.

◆ Bake until puffed and lightly browned, about 20 minutes. Cool at least 20 minutes or up to several hours.

◆ Carefully transfer the logs to a work surface and cut each crosswise into 20 slices. Return to the baking sheet.

◆ Bake for 12 minutes. Turn over and bake until the cookies are firm and lightly browned, 14–16 minutes longer. Transfer to wire racks to cool completely.

◆ Serve now, or store in a tightly covered container for up to 2 weeks.

index